The Writing Discovery Book

New Ways to Improve Writing Skills, Grades 4-8

David Clark Yeager

Scott, Foresman and Company
Glenview, Illinois
Dallas, Texas   Oakland, New Jersey
Palo Alto, California   Tucker, Georgia
London

More GOOD YEAR® Books in Language Arts and Reading

BASICS AND BEYOND
Practical Writing Activities for Today and Tomorrow
Michelle Berman and Linda Shevitz

BIG BOOK OF WRITING
Sandra Kaplan, Sheila Madsen, Bette T. Gould

DO YOU READ ME?
Practical Approaches to Teaching Reading Comprehension
Arnold A. Griese

GALAXY OF GAMES
For Reinforcing Writing Skills
Jerry Mallett

GETTING THE MOST OUT OF TELEVISION
Dorothy Singer, Jerome Singer, Diana M. Zuckerman

GETTING READY TO READ
Volume 1 and 2
Harry W. Forgan and M. Liz Christman-Rothlein

I CAN MAKE IT ON MY OWN
Functional Reading Ideas and Activities for Daily Survival
Michelle Berman and Linda Shevitz

IMAGINE THAT!
Illustrated Poems and Creative Learning Experiences
Joyce King and Carol Katzman

LANGUAGE ARTS IDEA BOOK
Classroom Activities for Children
Joanne Schaff

MAKING KIDS CLICK
Independent Activities in Reading and Language Arts
Linda Polon and Aileen Cantwell

ME? TEACH READING?
Activities for Secondary Content Area Teachers
Mary Beth Culp and Sylvia Spann

NEW DIMENSIONS IN ENGLISH
An Ideabook of Language Arts Activities for Middle and Secondary School Teachers
Joanne Schaff

OUNCE OF PREVENTION PLUS A POUND OF CURE
Tests and Techniques for Aiding Individual Readers
Ronald W. Burton

PHORGAN'S PHONICS
Harry W. Forgan

READ ALL ABOUT IT
Using Interests and Hobbies to Motivate Young Readers
Harry W. Forgan

READING CORNER
Ideas, Games, And Activities for Individualizing Reading
Harry W. Forgan

READING FOR SURVIVAL IN TODAY'S SOCIETY
Volumes I and II
Anne H. Adams, Anne Flowers, and Elsa E. Woods

READING ROUSERS
114 Ways to Reading Fun
Marian Bartch and Jerry Mallett

SPECIAL THINGS FOR SPECIAL DAYS
Pat Short and Billee Davidson

SUCCESS IN READING AND WRITING SERIES
Anne H. Adams, Elizabeth Bebensee, Helen Cappleman, Judith Connors, and Mary Johnson

TEACHER'S CHOICE
Ideas and Activities for Teaching Basic Skills
Sandra N. Kaplan, Sheila K. Madsen, and Bette T. Gould

TOTALACTION
Ideas and Activities for Teaching Children Ages Five to Eight
Pat Short and Billee Davidson

WRITE UP A STORM
Creative Writing Ideas and Activities for the Middle Grades
Linda Polon and Aileen Cantwell

WRITING CORNER
Arnold Cheyney

For information about these or other GOOD YEAR® Books, please write to

GOOD YEAR® Books
Scott, Foresman and Company
1900 East Lake Avenue
Glenview, Illinois 60025

ISBN: 0-673-15647-8

Copyright © 1983 Scott, Foresman and Company.

All Rights Reserved.

Printed in the United States of America.

123456-BKC-878685848382

Chases' Calendar of Annual Events by William D. Chase and Helen M. Chase (January — "'Proclaim Your Own Week' Week") used with permission of Apple Tree Press, Inc. P.O. Box Box 1012, Flint, Michigan 48501.

"The Zax" in *The Sneeches And Other Stories* by Dr. Seuss (March — "Solla Sollew To You") used with permission of Random House Inc., 201 East 50th Street, New York, New York 10022.

Table of Contents

		Page
Introduction		v

TITLE	ACTIVITY	ACADEMIC SUBJECT	

September

Roving Reporter	Interview	*Language Arts*	1
Captain's Log	Journal	*Language Arts*	3
Law Of The Land	Creating a Constitution	*Social Studies*	5
Navigator	Researching a Country	*World Geography*	7
Armchair Tourist	Requesting Information	*U.S. Geography*	9

October

Rules Of The Game	Developing Rules for Play	*Physical Education*	11
Trick Or Truth	Developing Questions and Answers	*Multidiscipline*	13
Brandon Blossom's Hocus-Pocus	Fiction — Characterization	*Language Arts*	15
The Grand Plan	Scale and Design	*Mathematics*	17
Noah Webster Was Right	Constructing a Dictionary	*Language Arts*	19

November

The Practical Pollster	Conducting an Opinion Poll	*Math/Social Studies*	21
Stringer's Solution	Fiction — Adventure	*Language Arts*	23
Red Hot Reading	Writing a Book Review	*Reading*	25
Sunday's Funnies	Cartooning	*Art/Language Arts*	27
Selling The Econocar	Creating a Brochure	*Science/Art*	29

December

A Whiplash Unbraiding In The Sun	Poetry	*Language Arts*	31
Equal Rights Under The Law	Specifying Rights	*Social Studies*	33
Supplies For Outpost One	Decision Making	*Social Studies/Math*	35
How The Lion Got His Mane	Storytelling	*Language Arts*	37

January

"Proclaim Your Own Week" Week	Writing a Proclamation	*Multidiscipline*	39
Ready To Read Recipes	Developing a Balanced Meal	*Math/Nutrition*	41
A Bit Of Braille	Coding and Decoding	*Math/Language Arts*	43

TITLE	ACTIVITY	ACADEMIC SUBJECT	

February

Tune Up Your Teeth	Making a Poster	*Health/Science*	45
Bright Ideas Can Light Up Your Life	Patenting an Invention	*Science*	47
Be A Weather Wizard	Writing a Weather Report	*Science*	49
Music With Morse	Writing Song Lyrics	*Music Composition*	51
Most Dangerous Mission	Fiction — Narrative	*Language Arts*	53

March

Awareness Helps	Researching — Endangered Animals	*Science/Social Studies*	55
Solla Sollew To You	Fiction — Beginning Reader Stories	*Language Arts*	57
Heads Up!	Conducting a Census	*Math/Social Studies*	59
Adopt An Artist	Researching and Writing a Biography	*Art/History*	61
How To Say NO!	Creating Dialogue	*Language Arts*	63

April

The Responsible Rider's Test	Making a Test	*Safety Education*	65
The North Pole Is Missing!	Fiction — Science Fiction	*Language Arts*	67
The Stranger Exchange	Writing Letters	*Language Arts*	69
Newsview: The Five O'Clock Report	Writing History As News	*Social Studies*	71
The Personal Prize	Establishing Criteria	*Multidiscipline*	73

May

"Elementary, My Dear Watson"	Fiction — Mystery	*Language Arts*	75
A Real Estate	Describing/Advertising	*Art/Language Arts*	77
Moms Abound	Composing and Designing a Greeting Card	*Language Arts/Art*	79
All Aboard!	Developing an Itinerary	*Geography/Mathematics*	81
All The Law Allows	Deciding a Legal Dispute	*Creative Dramatics*	83

June

Flags Aloft	Designing a Flag	*Art/Language Arts*	85
Flashdown!	Interpreting Data/ Summarizing	*Science*	87
A Summer Time Capsule	Recording Feelings and Ambitions	*Language Arts*	89

INTRODUCTION

Writing. That single word covers a multitude of activities — everything from making grocery lists to composing sonnets. Yet students (and some teachers) tend to think of writing as limited to the themes, essays, and stories required in a language arts curriculum. *The Writing Discovery Book* is designed to broaden student understanding and appreciation of writing as a form of communication that not only relates to other academic subjects but also permeates the "real world" outside the classroom.

Research indicates that quality writing depends on exposure to a variety of communication skills as well as guided practice in putting words on paper. Oral presentation, discussion, persuasion, decision-making, and appreciation of the visual arts all contribute to a student's development as a writer. The exercises presented in *The Writing Discovery Book* have been written to develop student skills in each of these areas, as well as in the traditional genres of fiction writing.

No writing program can be successful, however, unless students see it as relevant to their needs. In selecting specific annual events or dates of historical significance, *The Writing Discovery Book* allows the teacher to use the writing activity in conjunction with topical material in the academic areas of math, science, social studies, health, physical education, reading, and the other language arts. Students begin to recognize writing as a skill which can help them with all learning.

How To Use *The Writing Discovery Book*

The Table of Contents lists the title, the type of writing activity, and the academic discipline to which each exercise relates. You may wish to integrate the activity into your schedule to coincide with the most appropriate academic subject.

The pre-writing passages are succinct, usually requiring no more than ten minutes, including discussion. You may wish to read the selection orally to the class, or duplicate it, making available one classroom set for your students. The closing sentences of each selection lead into the writing instructions which are presented at the top of each activity page. These instructions have been written at a low intermediate reading level.

The writing activities can be completed in a single class session, although the length of each one has been left open to accommodate individual student differences. Most activities encourage the students to continue the assignment on regular lined paper after they have completed the duplicated assignment page. Several of the assignments, when completed, make excellent bulletin board displays or interest centers. Others can be bound and included in the school library as circulating student-prepared materials.

If you know of any annual events or significant dates in history that you might like to see included in a later edition of *The Writing Discovery Book,* please send them to Scott, Foresman and Company, 1900 East Lake Avenue, Glenview, IL 60025; c/o Christopher Jennison.

September

Roving Reporter

"The news of the world is coming up next. But first, a word from our sponsor..."

On the evening of September 20, 1921, hundreds of people in Pittsburgh, Pennsylvania tuned their radios to station KDKA. After a few opening commercials, the station began broadcasting the first regularly scheduled newscast in America.

During those early days of radio, reporters in the field would write their story and then read it over the telephone to an announcer at the station. A few reporters even used trained homing pigeons to fly their handwritten messages to the station. If the reporter was in another country, it might take several days for his news to reach the radio station. As more and more people began buying radios, news reporters tried to find better ways to do their job.

Today, the news is reported at the speed of light. Using microwave transmitters and satellites, the voice of a reporter in Germany can be broadcast directly to a radio audience as far away as California. A news director, with the help of his staff, can put together a news broadcast using reporters from almost every country in the world.

Sharpen your pencils and replace the batteries in your tape recorder. On the next page, you'll be doing a news report of your own.

did you know?

There are more than 400,000,000 radios in the United States today. Nearly one in every four is in an automobile.

Roving Reporter

Name _____

Roving Reporter

EDITORIAL COMMENT: A good radio interview should contain as many facts as possible. The reporter must think of questions the audience will want answered. Listeners certainly will want to know WHOM you are interviewing, WHAT kinds of things the person enjoys doing, and WHERE he or she enjoys spending time. A brief beginning outline will start you off on the right foot...

_____   _____
(name of person interviewed)   (person's favorite subject)

_____   _____
(person's favorite sport)   (person's favorite place)

_____   _____
(person's favorite food)   (person's least favorite food)

ASK FIVE QUESTIONS OF YOUR OWN:

_____
_____
_____
_____
_____

NOW THAT YOU HAVE ALL OF THE INFORMATION YOU NEED, WRITE YOUR OWN NEWS STORY, KEEPING YOUR AUDIENCE IN MIND.

_____
_____
_____
_____
_____ continue on your own paper.

September

September

Half Moon Captain's Log

Each year millions of people travel to and from one of the busiest islands in the world. Manhattan Island, the business center of New York City, must have looked much different to Henry Hudson as he sailed toward it on September 11, 1609.

Henry Hudson was an explorer hired by the Dutch East India Trading Company. The company wanted him to find a way to sail right through the center of North America. If such an inland passage could be found, it would save the trading company months of time. The Dutch East India Company specialized in bringing merchandise to Europe from the Far East. If the ships could sail through America instead of around it, they could bring Far East merchandise to Europe in record time.

Hudson never found an inland passage. We now know that no such waterway exists. But Hudson did discover Manhattan Island and the river beside it. Today, that river is named the Hudson in his honor. Although he didn't achieve his original goal, Henry Hudson did discover one of America's most important rivers and islands. As a result, he opened the way for even greater explorations in the New World.

take a look

Standing near the top of the Empire State Building on a clear day, you can sometimes see five states: New York, New Jersey, Pennsylvania, Connecticut, and Massachusetts.

Captain's Log

Captain's Log

Name _____

BEFORE YOU CAST OFF: Most successful explorers kept journals or diaries. You have been hired by the WEATHERALL TRADING COMPANY to explore an island recently discovered in the South Seas. You have just three days to hike around the island before writing your report. In your journal, you will want to make note of what the land is like (rocky? sandy?), what bodies of water you discovered (large lake? small but dangerous streams?), wildlife (any ferocious animals?), as well as the direction in which you traveled...

DAY 1: _____

_____

_____

_____

_____ continue on your own paper.

DAY 2: _____

_____

_____

_____

_____ continue on your own paper.

DAY 3: _____

_____

_____

_____

_____ continue on your own paper.

Now that you are safely back on your boat, draw a map of what your island would look like if you were to fly over it.

September

September

Law Of The Land

We the people of the United States, in order to form a more perfect union, establish justice, insure domestic tranquility, provide for the common defense, promote the general welfare, and secure the blessings of liberty to ourselves and our posterity (children), *do...establish this Constitution for the United States of America.*

These words form the preamble, or beginning, of the Constitution of the United States. On September 17, 1787, thirty-nine leaders of this country signed the Constitution. It became our national law when nine states approved it.

Many of the early states had already written and adopted their own constitutions; but this was the first time that the federal government had so carefully defined the laws of the entire country. The Constitution gave certain powers to the federal government, such as the power to maintain an army. Powers not given to the federal government belonged to the states and to the people.

The Constitution should be changed only when absolutely necessary. Since it first became our national law, the Constitution has been changed twenty-six times. Any change in the Constitution is called an amendment.

A constitution provides one way of allowing people to work out problems. If someone does something that is not allowed under a constitution, then the government can punish that individual. The Constitution is the most important document enacted by the United States Government.

Law Of The Land

Law Of The Land

Name _____

HERE YE, HEAR YE: You and four hundred passengers aboard the cruise ship *U.S.S. Behr* are suddenly jolted off your feet. The ship has run aground in a dense fog. There is no radio communication and no way to contact the outside world. Everyone immediately realizes that there must be some sort of order on board until help arrives. You are asked to write a constitution of just seven laws. Each law will be referred to as an "article." While writing your laws, think of the words freedom, justice, and equality. They should be of great help.

ARTICLE I. _____

ARTICLE II. _____

ARTICLE III. _____

ARTICLE IV. _____

ARTICLE V. _____

ARTICLE VI. _____

ARTICLE VII. _____

September

September

Navigator

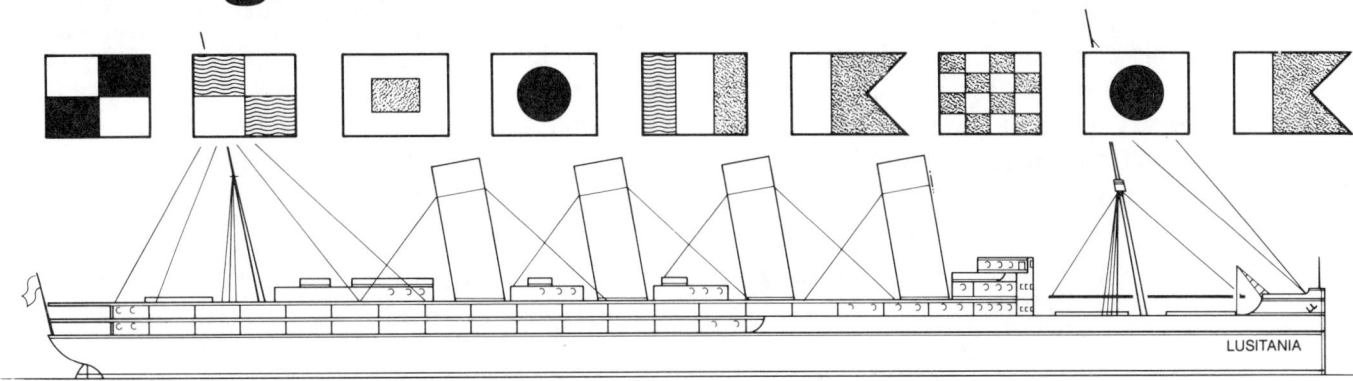

Flags similar to these were draped from the main stack of the luxury ship *Lusitania* as it steamed into New York harbor. The arrival of the ship on September 12, 1907 — just five days and fifty-four minutes after leaving England — set a new world's speed record for travel across the Atlantic Ocean.

The *Lusitania* is also remembered for the last voyage it ever made. In May of 1915, a German submarine sunk the great ship with a torpedo near the coast of Ireland. The sinking of the *Lusitania* was one of the reasons that the United States entered World War I.

Luxury ships still sail today. Although travelers in a hurry prefer the jet airplane, cruise ships take passengers to exciting and remote parts of the world that can't be reached by large jets. You can board ships that sail through the tropical South Seas. If you'd rather see icebergs, you can board a ship which sails north along the coast of Canada up to Alaska.

Seeing the world aboard a ship is a great adventure. On the next page you will embark on a trip around the world. Stop in a friendly port and learn something about the country. As the navigator, you will want to make a report to the captain.

there's more

The flags shown above spell out the ship's name, **Lusitania.** *Each flag design represents a different letter of the alphabet. The first flag, for example, represents the letter "L." The fourth and eighth flags represent the letter "I." For a complete explanation of ships flags, look under the entry FLAGS in your encyclopedia.*

Navigator

Navigator

Name _____

CAPTAIN'S COMMENTS: You have been hired to be the navigator aboard the *S.S. Sea Serpent*. Tomorrow we will sail from New York to any and all of the places you would like to see. There are just a few rules you must follow. The first rule is that we must sail to at least ten countries. The second rule is that we must change direction after each stop. If we sail northeast to Iceland, for example, we can sail in any direction but northeast after leaving Iceland. Make certain you complete the Navigator's Report below. Use an encyclopedia for help.

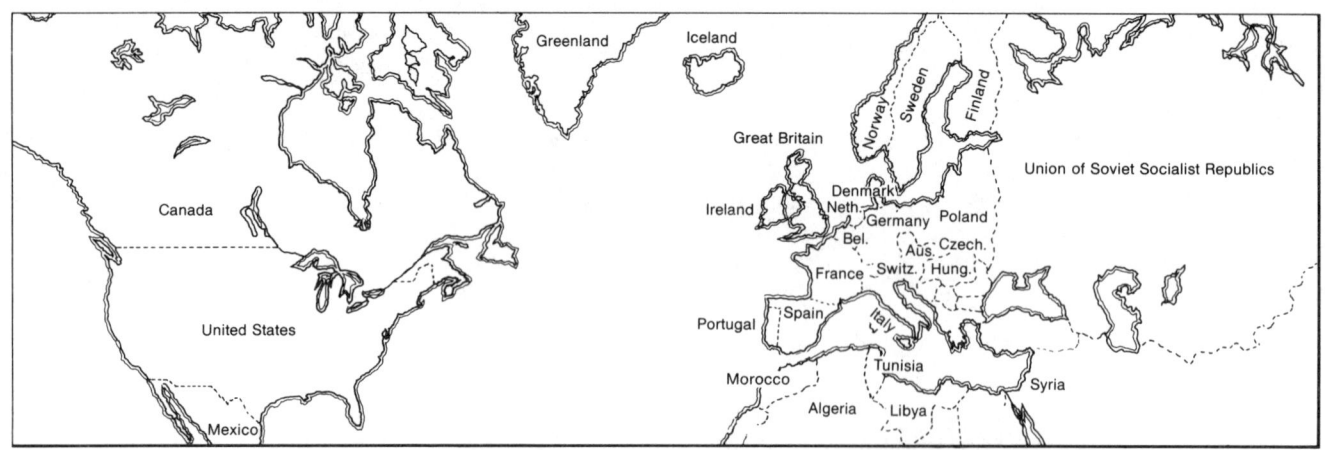

NAVIGATOR'S REPORT

COUNTRIES VISITED:

1. _____   2. _____   3. _____

4. _____   5. _____   6. _____

7. _____   8. _____   9. _____

10. _____

SELECT ONE COUNTRY FOR THIS PART OF THE REPORT

NAME OF COUNTRY _____   POPULATION _____

CAPITAL CITY _____   AREA (sq. miles) _____

What type of currency is in use? _____

What form of government is in power? _____

Who is the current ruler of the country? _____

What are the chief products of the country? _____

WRITE A DESCRIPTION OF THIS COUNTRY. YOU MIGHT WANT TO INCLUDE WHY YOU DECIDED TO STOP THERE.

September

September

Armchair Tourist

September is a month of automotive firsts. The first automobile parade left Newport, Rhode Island on September 7, 1899. Nineteen car fanciers from almost a dozen states traveled over narrow and often bumpy roads just to take part in the event.

If they had waited just fourteen years, the drivers of these cars might have traveled along part of the Lincoln Highway. Built at a cost of more than $10,000,000, the road officially opened on September 10, 1913, and stretched all the way from New York to California. The Lincoln Highway passed through thirteen states, over two mountain ranges, and across a stretch of desolate prairie land. Service stations and hotels were often difficult to find. But nothing stopped Neil Patterson. He became the first person to drive from one end of the Lincoln Highway to the other.

Today, major freeways connect ninety percent of the large cities in the United States. There are more than four million miles of highways, streets, and roads in the country. Because it's easy to get lost, it is just as important today to plan a trip carefully as it was when Neil Patterson drove the Lincoln Highway. Two adventuresome travelers from New Jersey can attest to that.

On September 9, 1976, a cab driver in Hoboken, New Jersey agreed to drive two passengers on their vacation. The passengers offered to pay the driver $2,500 for the entire trip. He accepted their offer, and the three set off on what would soon become the world's longest cab ride — passing through fifteen states! So get out your travel folders. You are about to become armchair tourists.

Armchair Tourist

Name _____

Armchair Tourist

TOURIST TIP: Most state governments have special offices which will mail information about their state to you. Look at a map of the United States. Do you see someplace that looks exciting? Perhaps there is a state that you have always wanted to visit. Write a letter to their Tourist Information Center, asking specifically for the kind of information you want. Follow the letter form outlined below, and write your letter on a clean sheet of lined paper.

_____
(date)

_____
(your name)

_____
(street address)

_____
(city, state, zip code)

Tourist Information Center

State of _____

_____
(city, state, zip code)

_____:

_____
_____
_____
_____
_____

Very truly yours,

(your signature)

September

October

Rules Of The Game

"The pitch is a fast ball. The batter swings and...he misses. That's the third out as we move to the bottom of the ninth inning."

On October 1, 1903, the Boston Pilgrims and the Pittsburgh Nationals played the first World Series baseball game. Boston, playing before a sellout crowd at their home stadium, went on to capture the Series five games out of eight.

Sports have always been important in this country. Many people use sporting activities to stay in good health. Walk through a park and you'll probably see people jogging, cycling, swimming, or playing a team sport like volleyball. Some team sports — such as football, soccer, and lacrosse — require much larger fields than you find in most parks.

Many of the games we play today were invented long ago in countries as far away as Ireland and China. Badminton, croquet, and rugby all came to this country from Europe or India. By playing games with people of other lands, we also learn how to communicate better with our neighbors.

Games and other forms of physical activity not only make you feel better, but they make you feel better about yourself. Now is the time to help others feel better, too. On the next page you will have the opportunity to design the game of a lifetime.

Rules Of The Game

Name _____

Rules Of The Game

TIME OUT: Last year, the people of the city decided they needed a new playing field in the park. Since they wanted it finished in a hurry, they hired five different companies to work on the field at the same time. Unfortunately, each company built a different kind of field. The result of this mess is shown below. Since the city is stuck with the strange field anyway, they decided to invent a new game to go with it. It is up to you to decide what type of equipment will be used in the game. You will also have to explain how a player can score in your game. If the player touches the ball, is he out? Or does he have to touch the ball to make a run? It's up to you to decide.

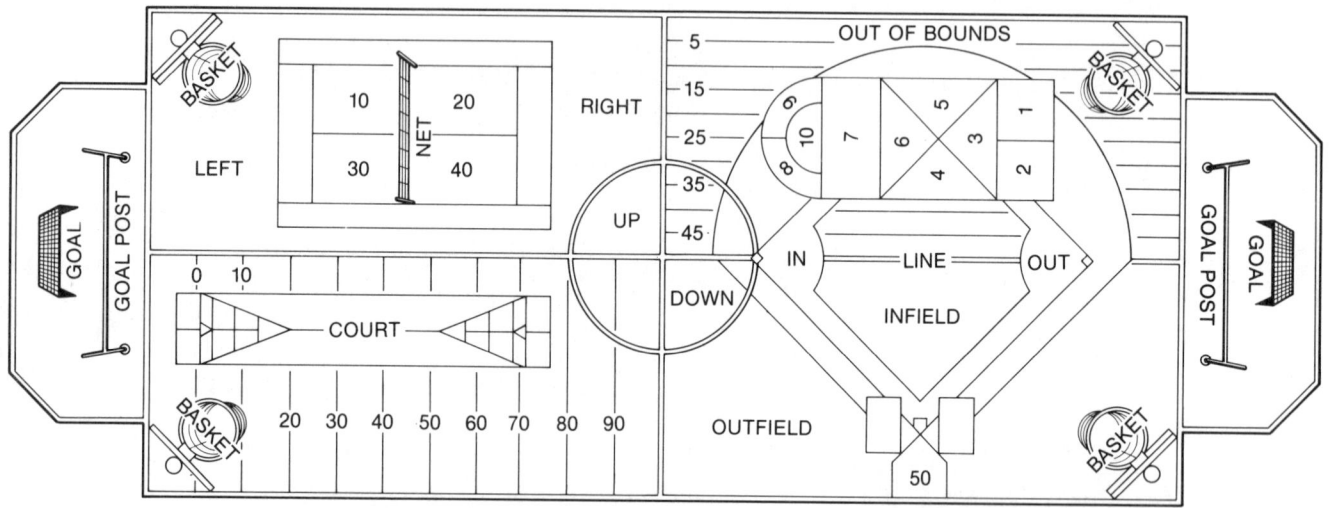

SUGGESTED EQUIPMENT: racquets, balls, nets, baskets, hoops, mallets, bats, sticks, gloves, mitts, goals, special shoes.

NAME OF THE GAME _____

EQUIPMENT NEEDED _____
_____

RULES OF THE GAME

1. _____
_____

2. _____

_____ continue on another sheet of paper.

October

October

Trick Or Truth

Approximately how many times a minute should a canary's heart beat?

Questions like the one above helped launch the successful radio and television career of one of America's best-known comedians. On October 27, 1947, Groucho Marx broadcast the first "You Bet Your Life" program. Groucho was know for his bushy black moustache, thick cigar, and outrageous humor. He asked contestants on the radio program a series of occasionally tricky but always funny questions. The show became so popular that it later became one of the first game shows on television.

People from all over the country came to watch the show in person in the hope of being selected to appear with Groucho Marx. Although "You Bet Your Life" eventually left the air, many more TV game shows have followed it.

In some cities, game shows make up more than twenty-four hours of each broadcast week. Many of the more successful shows have waiting lists of people requesting tickets for the program. Contestants must pass certain tests on some shows before they are allowed to appear before the TV cameras. Usually, the questions on these game shows are not too difficult to answer. But, once in a while, the host will ask a very difficult question.

Comb your hair and put on your best smile. You are about to become the host of "Trick Or Truth." But before you go on the air, you might like to know that a canary's heart beats approximately 1,000 times each minute!

Trick Or Truth

Name _____

Trick Or Truth

A WORD FROM THE SPONSOR: You've been hired as the new quizmaster on the national game show "Trick Or Truth." It is your job to prepare each question you ask. If the contestants can answer each of your questions, then they win. You can ask trick questions, but only if you know the correct answer. The encyclopedia, a world almanac, and a dictionary should be of help in preparing the questions.

CATEGORY: Sports
Sample: Who was Mildred "Babe" Didrikson Zaharias?
   A: Perhaps the greatest woman athlete in history

Q: _____
   A: _____
Q: _____
   A: _____
Q: _____
   A: _____

CATEGORY: States
Sample: How many miles of coastline does the state of Maine have?
   A: Approximately 3,500 miles of coastline

Q: _____
   A: _____
Q: _____
   A: _____
Q: _____
   A: _____

CATEGORY: Science
Sample: At what temperature does water freeze?
   A: Thirty-two degrees Fahrenheit

Q: _____
   A: _____

October

October

Brandon Blossom's Hocus-Pocus

Here is a short Halloween quiz:

OCHUS BOCHUS is:
1. The name of the headless horseman's village
2. An ingredient in Wicked Witch of the West's potion in the film *Wizard of Oz*
3. A wizard in ancient Norse folktales

Creeping goblins! It's hard to believe that October 31 is fast approaching. Since the early seventh century, people in all parts of the world have observed All Hallowed Eve, or Halloween, on the last day of the month. But not many people are aware that National Magic Day is observed at the same time.

In memory of the death of Harry Houdini on October 31, 1926, professional magicians spend the day holding meetings and demonstrations. By sharing the tricks of their trade and by helping younger performers develop the profession, the magicians feel they are doing what Houdini would have wanted.

Harry Houdini was probably the greatest magician that ever lived. An expert escape artist, he was able to free himself from tight-fitting handcuffs in seconds. Moments later, Houdini could find his way out of a locked trunk, carefully secured by chains. Harry Houdini never publicly divulged his secrets. He was often heard to say, however, that his tricks were so simple that any youngster could perform them.

Join with thousands of other professional and amateur magicians and celebrate National Magic Day. On the next page you will meet Brandon Blossom, one of the unlikeliest magicians around.

By the way, the correct answer to the quiz is number three. Ochus Bochus is a character from Norwegian folktales. Not surprisingly, his name is the root of the magician's term "Hocus-Pocus."

Brandon Blossom's Hocus-Pocus

EDITORIAL EDICT: Most people love to read fiction. Writers enjoy creating fiction by weaving characters and situations together in new, and often humorous, ways. They can change scenes, make the action pass quickly, and even make the impossible happen. You are about to read the first of the strange events that happened to Brandon Blossom. Brandon's story is only half finished, however. Using another sheet of paper, you will soon write the exciting conclusion to...

Brandon Blossom's Hocus-Pocus

Brandon spent most of the afternoon looking at the clock. When three o'clock finally arrived, he sprang from his desk and shot toward the door.

Tito Aquilar, his best friend, found himself running just to keep up. "Well, it's three o'clock. You said you'd tell me what you are going to wear to the Halloween Carnival tonight."

Brandon pulled seven dollars from his hip pocket. "I finally saved enough to buy that old suit of armor at Second Hand Roy's antique shop. I'm wearing that tonight."

But when they arrived at Second Hand Roy's, Brandon saw that the armor — which had been in the window of the shop for six months — was gone.

Brandon pushed open the warped front door of the shop. Nervously, he approached the thin, gray man sitting in the shady corner of the store.

"The armor is gone," the old man cackled with glee before Brandon had even asked his question. "But I have this cape and hat." He threw the cape at Brandon and began chanting, "Hocus-Pocus...out of focus."

Suddenly...

October

October

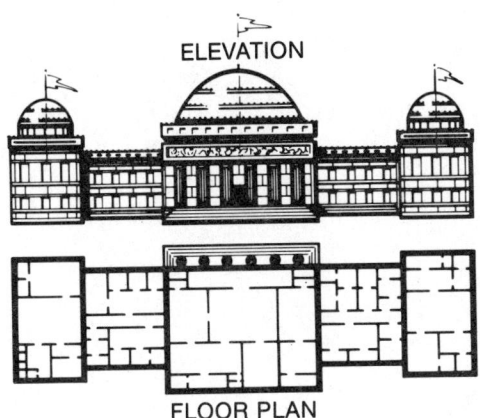

The Grand Plan

Thomas Jefferson, the third president of the United States, was also an architect. He entered the contest held to select the best design for the Executive Mansion (president's home). But when he submitted his design, Jefferson left his name off the plans so his true identity would not be revealed.

Thomas Jefferson may have been disappointed when his plans were not accepted. On October 13, 1792, architect James Hoban, the winner of the contest, began construction of the famous Washington, D.C. landmark.

It took almost eight years to complete the mansion. During the final months of the construction, Hoban ordered all of the outside walls of the building to be painted white. When President John Adams moved into the finished home in 1800, it was already known as the "White House." Unfortunately, when the mansion was just fourteen years old it had to be completely rebuilt.

During the War of 1812, British troops attacked our nation's capital, setting fire to the White House and several other government buildings. After the war, Hoban returned to supervise the reconstruction of the mansion. Since the reconstruction, the White House has been remodeled several times. In 1834, pipes were installed to bring fresh spring water into the house. Almost sixty years later, the White House was wired for electricity. In 1952, President Harry Truman and his family were asked to move out while the White House was completely repaired. The work cost several million dollars and took four years to complete, but when the job was finished the White House was just as sound as it was when John Adams first moved in.

Today's White House has 132 rooms (including private offices), a dining room that can seat 140 guests at one table, and even a small movie theater. So get out your blue paper and pencils. It's time for you to make a grand plan of your own.

The Grand Plan

The Grand Plan

Name _____

ARCHITECT'S ADVICE: The year is 2038, and a new country has recently been formed on the light side of the moon. King Luna Crater has asked you and several other architects to draw up plans for a new palace. According to the rules of the King's contest, each architect must design a house suitable for the King of the Moon, complete with every comfort a king might need. After you have finished the design, identify each room by name. Then write a description of your palace, explaining why it is the best design for the new King to choose.

THE KING'S PALACE DATE _____

DESIGN NUMBER _____ ARCHITECT _____

BEFORE DESIGNING YOUR ENTRY, PLEASE ANSWER THESE QUESTIONS:

1. How many rooms will this palace have? _____

2. How will the palace be heated?
   - ☐ solar
   - ☐ coal fires
   - ☐ gas
   - ☐ electric
   - ☐ other

3. What special inventions will be included in this palace? _____
   _____
   _____

4. Will there be any special rooms designed for exercise or recreation (indoor tennis courts, swimming pools, or bowling lanes)? If the answer is yes, list these rooms below:
   _____
   _____
   _____

5. What special entertainment rooms will be included in this palace?
   _____

6. List any other special features of your palace: _____
   _____

On an unlined piece of paper, complete the design of your palace. Then continue on lined paper, writing the complete description of your palace. Be sure to include the reasons why it should be accepted by the King.

October

October

Noah Webster Was Right

INEXPENSIVE   CHEAP

Noah Webster, the well-known American educator and writer, was born on October 16, 1758. After graduating from Yale College, Webster began studying to become a lawyer. Webster did practice law, but not for very long. His love of words and his fascination with language led Webster into education. While teaching he wrote one of the first spelling books, a widely used grammar book, and finally a reading book for his students to use.

As he worked on these projects, Noah Webster began collecting words. Whenever he ran across a word he'd never read or heard before, he would record its proper spelling, pronunciation, and meaning. By October of 1828, he had put the finishing touches on the largest dictionary he had ever compiled. Titled *An American Dictionary of the English Language*, it was first published in November 1828. Included in the book were thousands of words and definitions that had never before appeared in a dictionary.

There are more than 400,000 English-language words in use today. Many of the words have similar definitions, or meanings. But even when two words mean almost the same thing, they might not always form the same image in your mind. For example, think about the words "cheap" and "inexpensive." Their definitions are similar. But if you bought a watch on sale, would you rather tell people it was a cheap watch or an inexpensive watch?

Get out a ballpoint pen, or stylus. You will soon have a chance to write *The First Dictionary of Unknown Words*.

did you know?

The word most often used in the English language is "I."

Noah Webster Was Right

Noah Webster Was Right

Name_____

WISE WORDS WEBSTER MIGHT HAVE SAID: A dictionary is a writer's most often used book. A dictionary not only provides the correct spelling and pronunciation of a word, but it also lets the writer know how a word should be used. In addition, a dictionary lists the ways in which a word can change in both number and tense. In the lists of verbs and nouns below, create your own words to fit the definitions provided. Then, using your own language, write and illustrate the last frame of the cartoon.

VERBS/
ACTION WORDS (Example: "Huph" in your language might mean "run" in English.)

YOUR LANGUAGE	ENGLISH
	sleep
	learn
	write
	stay

NOUNS/
WORDS NAMING PEOPLE, PLACES, OR THINGS

YOUR LANGUAGE	ENGLISH
	school
	home
	night
	day
	answer
	question
	me
	you

LIST BELOW ANY OTHER WORDS YOU MAY NEED

October

November

The Practical Pollster

Do you feel there is too much sugar added to breakfast cereals?

How many days a week do you eat new Choco-Chopper cereal?

Don't be too surprised if someone walks up to you asking questions similar to these. The person asking the questions is called a pollster, or interviewer. By answering the pollster's questions, you will become part of a national sample. By asking the same questions in several parts of the country, pollsters are able to find out how the entire nation feels about everything from peanut butter to politics.

Business leaders, news reporters, politicians, and even government officials use public opinion polls. Businesses use them to predict the success of products they offer for sale. The government conducts opinion polls to discover what effects certain laws will have on the nation. Candidates running for office may use the opinion poll to determine their chances of winning.

Sometimes public opinion polls are wrong and do not reflect how the people feel. This is exactly what happened in November 1948. Nearly every public opinion poll indicated that President Harry S. Truman would lose the election. But when the final votes were counted, the President had been re-elected by more than two million votes.

Since that time, public opinion polls have become more successful in predicting how people feel. Today, pollsters usually ask two types of questions — open and closed. An open question asks for an opinion, such as "Do you feel there is too much sugar...." Closed questions, such as "How many days a week do you eat new Choco-Chopper?" requires a specific answer from just a few choices. Practice your posture; you are about to become The Practical Pollster.

The Practical Pollster

Name _____

The Practical Pollster

THE OPINION OF A PUBLIC OPINION POLLSTER: You have recently been asked by all of the major television networks to determine which television programs are the most popular. You must ask at least seven people the same questions. To keep your sample accurate, you will want to ask people of different ages, of different interests, and in different classes in school. Sample open and closed questions appear below. You must supply the choices for question three. Then write an open question for number four and a closed question for number five.

1. (closed) HOW OLD ARE YOU? _____

2. (open) WHAT KIND OF TELEVISION PROGRAM DO YOU LIKE TO WATCH MOST OFTEN? _____

3. (closed) OF THE FOLLOWING, WHICH SHOW DO YOU WATCH MOST OFTEN?

    ☐ _____

    ☐ _____

    ☐ _____

4. (open) QUESTION: _____

    _____

    ANSWER: _____

    _____

5. (closed) QUESTION: _____

    _____

    ANSWER: _____

    ☐ _____

    ☐ _____

    ☐ _____

WHEN YOU'VE FINISHED THE PUBLIC OPINION POLL: Use another sheet of paper to discuss the following questions:

1. What conclusions can you draw about the kind of television programs people watch most often?

2. How can you show that your conclusions are based on a proper sample?

November

November
Stringer's Solution

The first cats in America were brought from Europe around 1725. More than 250 years later, there are 23,000,000 cats on this continent.

In honor of these millions of cats, the American Feline Society has proclaimed the first week of November to be Cat Week International. In recognition of the value of felines to the world, the Society encourages exhibitions on the proper care of cats, as well as cat shows and competitions.

Cats have been respected by people for thousands of years. The ancient Egyptians thought of the cat as a sacred creature. They carved statues and jewelry to resemble cats. Sailors, exploring uncharted waters, believed that having a cat on board ship brought good luck. A few people even believe the old superstition that cats have nine lives and that they can use their extra lives to protect their human owners.

Cats may not have nine lives, but they do have great agility and perseverance. In 1973, a cat fell from the twentieth floor of a Montreal, Canada building to the pavement below. Miraculously, the cat survived, suffering just one broken bone. There are also reports of cats traveling great distances to be reunited with former owners. In one case, a lost cat traveled all the way from San Francisco back to his home in Oklahoma. Aside from some scratches and obvious fatigue, the wandering cat suffered no serious effects from the 1,400-mile trip.

There may be no better way to celebrate Cat Week International than by writing a death-defying conclusion to the action adventure of a six-year-old tomcat.

Stringer's Solution

Stringer's Solution

HOW TO HELP A HERO: Adventure stories are one popular style of fiction. When writing an adventure, the author will usually develop several different challenges for his hero to face. Then, at the end of the book, the hero somehow overcomes all of the challenges and saves the day. Adventure story heroes come in a variety of forms. Heroes have been horses, dogs, and even Volkswagen automobiles. In this story, "Stringer's Solution," the hero is a friendly but gruff tomcat named Stringer. Read the beginning paragraphs of the story. Then, using your own paper, continue the story. Remember to save some of the action for the conclusion, where the hero solves everything.

Stringer walked quickly down Broadway, stopping every few feet to look inside each of the small shops that lined the street. At each door, the storekeepers left small saucers of milk or water. Stringer was just about to leave Giuseppe's Italian Market when he was startled by the sudden ringing of bells.

Most of the neighborhood dogs began barking and running in every direction. People on the street stopped to look toward the entrance of the McDonald office building. As more people ran into the street, flames began shooting from the windows of the restaurant on the first floor of the McDonald building.

"Fire!" Chef Pierre shouted as he ran from the restaurant kitchen. He was so excited that he ran right into a car parked at the corner.

The man sitting in the car was so surprised he pulled his hat down over his eyes and then sped away from the curb. Just as he left, three men wearing masks ran from the bank shouting, "Hey! Wait for us."

Behind the masked men, two uniformed bank guards ran into the street. "Stop! Thieves!" they shouted. But because they were so interested in stopping the robbers, the guards did not look where they were going. Just as they ran into the street, a large moving van turned the corner right behind them. If someone didn't do something, the truck driver would certainly not have time to stop.

Stringer knew it was time for him to act. Quickly, he...

November

November

Red Hot Reading

Hans Christian Andersen once read these words after they appeared in a review of his writing. "(Andersen's tales are) ...unsuitable for children (and)... harmful for the mind."

Hans Christian Andersen, the successful author of such highly praised tales as *The Ugly Duckling* and *The Emperor's New Clothes*, shouldn't have worried about this book reviewer's opinion. Many of Andersen's stories are more popular with children and adults today than they were more than a hundred and fifty years ago. Since this one uncomplimentary review appeared, hundreds of others have been published praising Andersen's unmatched skill as a storyteller.

November is the best month to look for reviews of good young adult and children's literature. The third week of November is traditionally recognized as Children's Book Week, sponsored by the Children's Book Council. During the week newspapers, libraries, and schools across the country highlight some of the best children's literature available. Other special activities include authors of children's books coming to local bookstores and schools to autograph books and talk with their readers. It has always been the readers that have made Children's Book Week so successful.

Today, there are more books available for children than at any other time in our history. You can help make this year's observance of Children's Book Week more successful by selecting one or two of these books and writing a short review of your own. If your local paper doesn't already publish reviews of children's books, offer yours. You might just find yourself featured as a guest writer for Children's Book Week.

Red Hot Reading

Name _____

Red Hot Reading

RULES FOR REVIEWERS: A review is a good way to let others know just how good (or bad) a particular book is to read. A reviewer of books has certain things he or she looks for when judging a book. These ways of judging a book are called "criteria." Below you will find several questions which will help you decide whether or not a book should be considered worthwhile reading. Use these criteria to write your book review. When you have finished the review, use a large sheet of drawing paper to create a poster advertising the book — similar to the posters used to advertise movies.

Title of book _____

Author _____

Publisher _____ Date published _____

Number of pages _____

Is the book fiction or nonfiction? _____

Are the illustrations appealing and colorful? _____

Are the characters in the book believable? _____

Describe the characters (include their appearance, age, and behavior):

_____

_____

Where does the story take place? _____

When does the story take place? _____

Why do you think the author wrote this book? _____

_____

_____

Did the author achieve his or her purpose? _____

How well did you like the book?

```
0      1      2      3      4      5           6      7      8      9      10
not at                            it was                                  very
all                               somewhat                                much
                                  enjoyable
```

Use this information to write your book review on another sheet of paper.

November

November
Sunday's Funnies

Which section of the newspaper is the most often read?

☐ National news
☐ Sports
☐ Comics
☐ Classified advertising

According to national surveys, the most popular newspaper section carries almost no news. It's the comic pages. The first Sunday comic pages in color date back to November 18, 1893. On that day, *The New York World* newspaper ran a humorous strip titled "Hogan's Alley" by Richard Outcault. The main character in the comic was a small, bald character known as the "yellow kid" because of his bright yellow clothing. "Hogan's Alley" became an overnight success. In just a few months other comic strips began appearing in newspapers all across the country.

Another famous cartoon character made his debut on November 18. In 1928 Mickey Mouse starred in the first talking movie cartoon, *Steamboat Willie.* Walt Disney, the creator of the cartoon mouse, used his own voice for Mickey's in the film. Mickey Mouse soon spread to comic books, newspaper comics, and later to television. Today, Mickey Mouse cartoons appear in several different languages.

Cartoons and comics became known as "funnies" because they were written to make people laugh. Most comics are still humorous, but a new type of cartoon has become popular. Private detectives, fearless knights, and space travelers now share the comic pages with the more humorous people and animals. It seems certain that comics will continue to grow in popularity. So get your drawing pens ready. This may be your chance to become the next Richard Outcault or Walt Disney.

Name _____

Sunday's Funnies

CARTOONIST'S COMMENTS: Many cartoonists feel that a comic strip is one of the most difficult assignments they face. In addition to drawing the necessary action, comic strip cartoonists must also write all of the necessary dialogue. To be able to do both of these tasks within six small frames often takes a great deal of planning. Below are six empty cartoon frames. After spending a few minutes thinking about your favorite cartoon characters, begin writing and illustrating your own comic strip. Remember, you are designing a Sunday comic. Therefore, when you have finished, your comic strip should be in full color.

November

November

Selling The Econocar

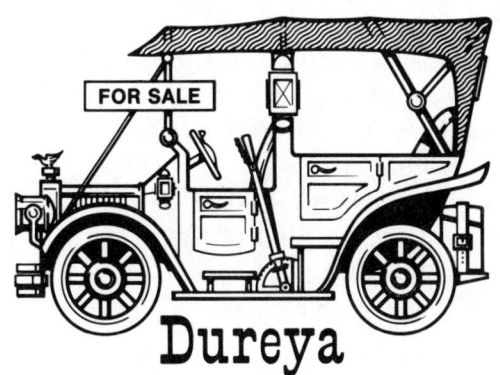

Imagine seeing this advertisement today:

The Dureya Motor Wagon is available now. $1,000 for the two seat model; $2,000 for the four seat deluxe model. This car has two motors and costs just ½¢ a mile to operate.

Today, the Dureya Motor Wagon would certainly help relieve the energy shortage. Unfortunately, this particular car has not been available for more than eighty years. The Dureya Motor Coach Company was in business near the turn of the century, a time when automobiles were beginning to replace the horse and buggy.

So popular were automobiles becoming during this period that the first automobile show opened on November 3, 1900. Sponsored by the Automobile Club of America, the show was held in New York City's Madison Square Garden. More than fifty automobile manufacturers set up booths at which they advertised their cars. Those companies unable to bring vehicles to the show distributed free sales brochures. Each manufacturer tried to show how much better the automobile was compared to the old-fashioned horse drawn carriage.

Some manufacturers even constructed steep ramps to demonstrate how well the automobile could climb. Others designed tight mazes to prove that their cars could be steered safely and reliably. The sales brochures and demonstrations were successful. Soon automobiles began appearing in every major city across the country.

Today, manufacturers sell their cars from showrooms. Although demonstration ramps and mazes are long gone, the sales brochure is still given to every interested customer. You are soon to become the chief design engineer for the new Econocar. Your first job will be to design the sales brochure. Good luck and good driving!

Selling The Econocar

Selling The Econocar

ENGINEERING REQUIREMENTS: You have been hired to design the new fuel-efficient, ultra-safe Econocar. You may design the car in any way you wish as long as you follow two basic rules. First, the car must be built in such a way as to get at least 75 miles per gallon of fuel. Second, the car must be loaded with safety equipment, making it impossible for passengers to be injured in an accident. In your illustration, label all of the fuel-saving and safety features you have included in your Econocar. Then, write a complete description of the car, convincing the reader that he or she should purchase your new vehicle. You will need at least one additional sheet of paper.

This is the new Econocar...

...and these are the reasons it should be your new vehicle.

CONTINUE ON YOUR OWN PAPER.

November

December

A Whiplash Unbraiding In The Sun

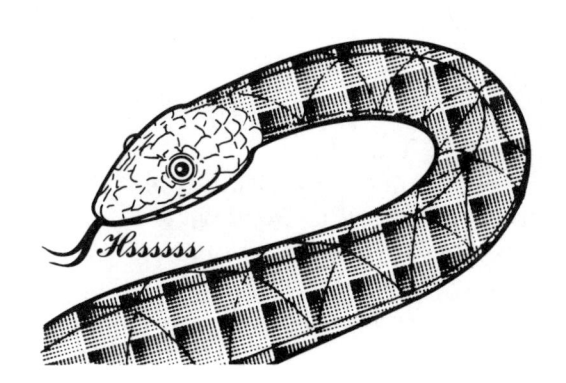

There's a certain slant of light,
Winter afternoons
That oppresses, like the weight
Of Cathedral tunes.

The woman who wrote this striking poem about nature rarely left her home and seldom in her life traveled beyond the border of her home state of Massachusetts. Emily Dickinson, one of the greatest American poets, was born December 10, 1830. Although her poems were short, usually only four-line stanzas, they clearly showed her appreciation for the quality of nature.

Dickinson spent much of her life at home reading and writing. She was uncomfortable in public, and she dreaded having to travel. She was shy at home, too. If guests called, she would have them sit in one room while she would sit in another, speaking to them through the door. While she found it difficult to communicate with others, Dickinson would occasionally write letters in the form of poems to her friends. A few of these poems were later published in short collections of her works.

At the time of her death, Dickinson had written over 1,775 poems, many of them unfinished and most without titles. She wrote in a strong style, using question marks and exclamation marks freely in her poetry. Many lines of her poetry ended with dashes — not a common style during her life. But Emily Dickinson wrote for herself, to express her feelings about life and nature. She was not interested in selling her poetry for publication. In fact, only seven of her poems were published before her death. Find a few other examples of Emily Dickinson's poetry. When you are familiar with her strength and style, try to create your own poetic expression about nature.

A Whiplash Unbraiding In The Sun

Name _____

A Whiplash Unbraiding In The Sun

A POET'S PURPOSE: The title of this activity is actually a description of a snake. Dickinson wrote the line after spending time in her garden, reflecting on nature. When she wrote, Dickinson experimented with different punctuation. Many of her poems contained questions or exclamations. She also experimented with the words she used. Many times she used "approximate rhymes" — two words that have similar sounds but don't quite rhyme (spar/despair). Write short poems, using a rhythm style that is comfortable for you, for the subjects listed below.

Winter

_____

_____

_____

A Heavy Rain

_____

_____

_____

Traveling Through A Dense Forest

_____

_____

_____

Now, using your own paper, write a poem describing your favorite part of nature.

December

December

Equal Rights Under The Law

**Thank you,
James Madison**

December 15 has always been an important date in U.S. history. On this date in 1791, the first ten amendments to the United States Constitution became law. That seemingly simple act guaranteed each of us the personal rights and freedoms which are this country's true national treasure.

When the Constitution was written, there were just thirteen states in the Union. Many of these states objected to the new Constitution, arguing that the document did not guarantee certain rights to every individual. James Madison, who later became the fourth president of this country, led the fight to amend (change) the Constitution to include guarantees of these rights. When the states approved the ten amendments, what people called "The Bill of Rights" became the law of the land.

Among other things, the Bill of Rights guarantees you the right to speak freely, the right to practice the religion of your choice, and the right to form groups or clubs. The First Amendment gives newspapers the right to print truthful articles about the government without fear of censorship.

Without these and the other freedoms guaranteed by the Bill of Rights, the United States might be a much different country. It took plenty of careful thinking by Madison and the other representatives to create the Bill of Rights. Imagine that you, today, are just beginning a new country. What rights would you guarantee your citizens? How would you protect the strength of your country? You will soon have the opportunity to answer these questions — and more — as you write your own Bill of Rights.

Name _____

Equal Rights Under The Law

WRITING ABOUT RIGHTS: The Bill of Rights is more than a collection of laws. The Bill of Rights speaks about the freedoms you enjoy as a citizen or visitor within the United States. Not one of these freedoms can be taken away from you. Imagine that you are starting a new country. What rights would you give yourself? What rights would you give to the people living under your rule? First, make a list of all of the rights you would like to see enacted in your country. Then, after giving your list some thought, explain how you would protect these rights if someone (or some other country) tried to take them away.

THE SECOND GREAT BILL OF RIGHTS

1. _____
   _____

2. _____
   _____

3. _____
   _____

4. _____
   _____

5. _____
   _____

How would you defend your rights if someone tried to take them from you?
_____
_____
_____
_____ continue on other paper.

December

December

Supplies For Outpost One

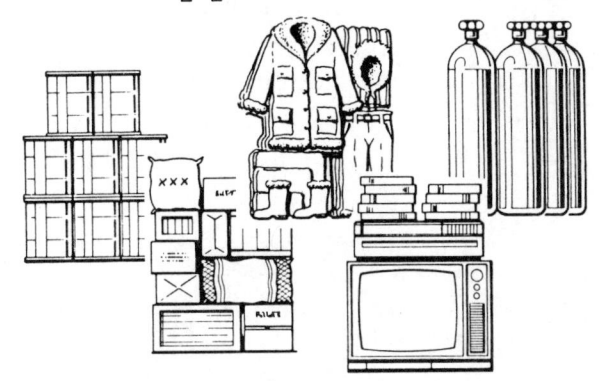

When the Norwegian explorer Roald Amundsen said good-bye to his family and friends in 1910, they all thought he was off on an exploration of the North Pole. Just over a year later — on December 14, 1911 — Amundsen became the first man to set foot on the South Pole!

While you might at first think that Mr. Amundsen had become quite confused and set sail in the wrong direction, Amundsen knew exactly what he was doing. Just as he was about to set out for the North Pole, he learned that another explorer — Admiral Robert Peary of the United States — had just become the first man to reach the North Pole. Amundsen also discovered that another explorer, Captain Robert Scott of England, was planning to sail soon for the South Pole. Amundsen knew that a trip to the North Pole would not be a first, and he decided to sail for the South Pole instead. Without announcing any change in his plans, Amundsen sailed from Norway, leaving everyone with the impression that he was sailing north.

Since Amundsen's first trip, there have been several expeditions to the South Pole. The United States, Japan, and the Soviet Union are among the countries that have established research stations on Antarctica. Scientists work year round studying the ice floes and the strange geological formations that make up this frozen continent.

Careful planning and preparation must go into every scientific expedition. Each explorer must have just the right equipment. Too much equipment would be heavy and dangerous to carry over the treacherous ice. Too little gear would leave the explorers to face severe hardships when faced with an Antarctic storm. You will soon be making some difficult decisions as you prepare for the last exploration from Outpost One.

Supplies For Outpost One

35

Supplies For Outpost One

Name _____

A DANGEROUS DIRECTIVE: You and a small group of scientists have been assigned to work inside Antarctic Outpost One for the next three months. You may take anything you want from the Exploration Command Storeroom below, but you must observe two rules. First, you may not take more than 310 kilograms (kg.) of supplies. And second, you must fully explain why you are taking each item that you select. You may use this form and another sheet of paper to request your supplies and explain your need of them.

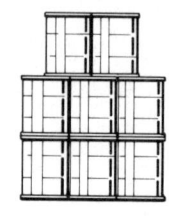

1 month water supply 50 kg.

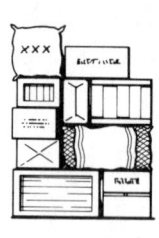

1 month food supply 50 kg.

clothing for 1 month 40 kg.

entertainment movies on videotape; each tape weighs 5 kg.; the machine weighs 10 kg.

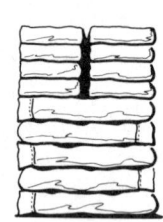

blankets and sheets; each pack lasts 1 month and weighs 20 kg.

books and magazines; each box weighs 5 kg.

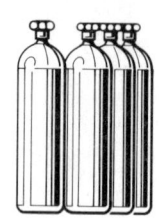

oxygen tanks; each tank will last one month and weighs 40 kg.

YOU MAY ORDER MORE THAN ONE OF EACH ITEM

ORDER FORM			
Quantity	Description of item	Weight of each	Total weight

On the following lines, explain why you chose what you did.

_____

_____ continue on another sheet of paper.

December

Copyright © 1983 Scott, Foresman and Company

December

How The Lion Got His Mane

How did the elephant get his trunk?

Why did the leopard grow spots?

Almost anyone can describe the way each of these animals appears. But it took British storyteller Rudyard Kipling's imagination to explain *why* they look the way they do. Born on December 30, 1865, Kipling grew up in both India and England. Upon graduation from school, he began a career as a newspaper reporter.

It was while working as a reporter that Kipling began writing his still-popular short stories. In many of his tales for children, Kipling wrote in a light, humorous style. Much of his writing has a definite rhythm and often contains repeated words designed to make young children laugh. While this style of writing was popular in short stories, it was not appreciated by his newspaper editors. It was not long before he left his newspaper job and devoted all of his time to writing and publishing his own stories.

Like many other writers of his time, Kipling also illustrated his own stories. In his most popular collection, *Just So Stories,* his illustrations seem to jump off the page. Children who have not yet learned to read the stories enjoy the book for its fascinating pictures. Two other books Kipling wrote and illustrated are *The Jungle Book* and *The Second Jungle Book.* In these two volumes, which are still popular today, Kipling describes the life of a young boy left in the jungle to be raised by a family of wolves. Mowgli, the boy in the story, learned his lessons from nature as did the elephant and leopard.

So find a safari hat and get ready. You are about to write a story of your own. By the way, the elephant — according to Kipling — had his trunk lengthened by a crocodile. The leopard grew his spots so that he could hide in the bushes without being seen.

How The Lion Got His Mane

Name _____

How The Lion Got His Mane

SUGGESTIONS FOR STORYTELLERS: Children who have not yet learned to read can still enjoy listening to the strange and funny tales of Rudyard Kipling. When writing a story that is to be told aloud, an author uses words that rhyme with one another. Then, when the story is presented aloud, the storyteller can use those words to make the story come alive by repeating them, or speaking them in a different tone of voice. On this page is an outline to help you get started on your story, "How the Lion Got His Mane." After you've completed the outline, use other paper to write your story. As Kipling did, you might want to supply your own illustrations. You may also want to check out some of Kipling's books from the library before writing your story.

BRAINSTORMING:

What are some words that rhyme with lion? _____
_____

What are some words that rhyme with mane? _____
_____

Where do most lions reside? _____

What kind of weather do you suppose lions must live in most of the time? _____

What possible reasons might a lion have for getting a mane such as the one he has? _____

If you were a lion, why would you want a mane? _____
_____

Some people think the lion is the king of the jungle. Might that have something to do with the size of his mane? _____

Now that you have answered these questions, you should be ready to start writing on your own. When you've finished, you might want to read your story and share your illustrations with one of the younger classes in your school.

December

January

"Proclaim Your Own Week" Week

Where in the world is the annual Bean Throwing Festival?

When do we observe National Grandparents Day?

What day has been set aside to honor "Wrong Way" Corrigan, the pilot who landed in Ireland while believing he'd just flown nonstop from New York to California?

These events, and thousands of others, are observed each year either because of their historical importance or because some group wanted to set aside a special day to recognize a special event. Whatever the reason for observing these special days, someone had to issue a proclamation establishing the observance. The first week of January is therefore proclaimed "Proclaim Your Own Week" week. All of us should use the week to remember those things in life that are important to us.

A proclamation is simply a public announcement that a certain period of time has been set aside to recognize someone or something. Anyone can issue a proclamation, although some proclamations are more official than others. The President of the United States proclaims some events, such as National Grandparents Day. Congress, governors, and state legislatures also issue special-events proclamations.

Private organizations also issue proclamations. The Unicorn Hunters Society of Michigan, for example, proclaims a full week in January as "Silent Record Week." By making this proclamation, the Society hopes everyone will remember the virtues of silence.

For more than twenty-five years, thousands of these special days and weeks have been listed in *Chases' Calendar of Annual Events*. According to this book, the Bean Throwing Festival is held in Japan, Grandparents Day is the first Sunday after Labor Day, and "Wrong Way" made his famous flight on July 17.

Now it's your turn to proclaim to everyone across the country that the first week in January should be set aside to honor something important to you.

"Proclaim Your Own Week" Week

Name _____

"Proclaim Your Own Week" Week

PROCLAMATION POINTERS: Proclamations have been issued for centuries. Many of the early proclamations were written on long sheets of paper rolled into scrolls. People still use scrolls today when they want to add a bit of creativity to their proclamations. But a proclamation can just be a simple announcement rather than a fancy scroll. Decide what or whom it is you wish to honor this week, and complete the following proclamation.

A PROCLAMATION

Be it known by all people that the first week in January is hereby proclaimed to be _____

_____

It is important to recognize _____

_____ this week for the following reasons:

A. _____

_____

_____

B. _____

_____

_____

C. _____

_____

_____

The following activities should be carried out this week in honor of this proclamation (list any special projects, activities, or field trips that might be conducted to make this proclamation even more meaningful):

1. _____
2. _____
3. _____

Signed _____

January

January

Ready To Read Recipes

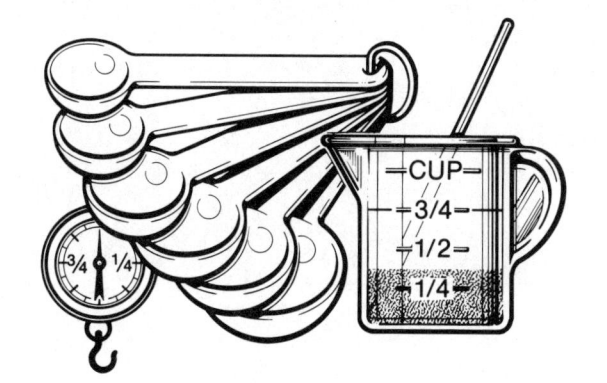

Here is a basic cooking test:

Start with a scoop of flour. Add a bit of baking powder, a shake or two of salt, just a touch of sugar, a smidgeon of cooking oil, a couple of eggs, and some milk...

Are you preparing
☐ waffles   ☐ paste   ☐ both

It seems hard to believe that at one time most recipes might have been written like the one above. Standard measures such as teaspoons, tablespoons, and the graduated measuring cup had not yet come into general use. But thanks to gourmet cook Fannie Farmer and her cookbook — first published in January of 1896 — recipes today are much easier to follow.

Fannie Farmer was a Boston, Massachusetts cooking instructor. She had her own school, Miss Farmer's School of Cookery. Through her experience in teaching kitchen organization and cooking to housekeepers and professional chefs, she was able to write *The Boston Cooking School Cookbook*. Still available today, her cookbook has become one of the most popular books of all time.

Publication of her cookbook also earned Fannie Farmer the title, "Mother of the Level Measurement." Just about every cookbook in existence today uses the same measurements Miss Farmer used in her original recipes.

Without level measurements, the recipe at the top of the page could turn out to be either paste or waffle batter. Keep that in mind as you write your own, easy-to-understand recipe.

Ready To Read Recipes

Name _____

Ready To Read Recipes

COMMENTS FROM A COOK'S KITCHEN: Most good cooks agree that a balanced meal should have some foods from each of these groups: vegetables and fruits; grains (breads and cereals); milk and cheese; and the protein group consisting of meat, poultry, fish, and beans. You have been asked to plan a meal for the 3,000 members of the Good Food Association of New England. Using the menu planner below, first list as many foods as you can for each of the groups. Then, using your imagination, write a recipe for a nutritious dessert to serve to the members. Avoid using foods high in fats and sugars.

VEGETABLES AND FRUITS: _____
_____
_____

GRAINS: _____
_____

MILK AND CHEESE: _____
_____

PROTEIN (MEAT, POULTRY, ETC.) GROUP: _____
_____
_____

USE SOME OF THE FOOD ITEMS YOU LISTED ABOVE TO PLAN YOUR DESSERT. REMEMBER TO USE PROPER MEASUREMENTS. SOME OF THE MEASURES YOU MIGHT WANT TO USE ARE:

Tablespoon (Tbs.)   teaspoon (tsp.)   cup   pint   pound
Each of these can be broken into fractional parts (½ pint, ¼ pound, for example).

RECIPE TITLE _____

List the ingredients needed for this recipe: _____
_____
_____

DESCRIBE EXACTLY THE WAY THIS RECIPE SHOULD BE PREPARED _____
_____ USE ANOTHER PAGE.

January

January

A Bit Of Braille

happy birthday, braille

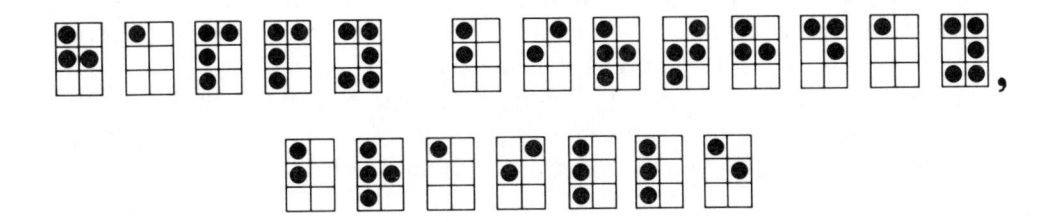

If the dots shown above were raised, anyone knowing the Braille alphabet would immediately know it said, "Happy Birthday, Braille."

Louis Braille, the designer of the Braille alphabet, was born in France on January 4, 1809. When he was quite young, a serious accident permanently blinded him. Only after several years of training was Braille able to attend school. When he was ten, his parents enrolled him in the National Institute for the Blind in Paris. It did not take long before Louis became an excellent student, especially in the areas of science and music. After only a few years of practice, Braille became an organist in a Paris church.

Following his graduation from the Institute, Braille chose to stay on as a teacher of other blind students. It was while he was an instructor that Braille came upon the idea of developing an alphabet that blind people could read easily. Braille set out to design an alphabet that could be read with the fingers. Using a system of raised dots, Braille assigned a combination of dots for each letter of the alphabet.

Today, newspapers, magazines, and books are published in the Braille alphabet. In 1961, *The World Book Encyclopedia* was translated into Braille. The finished work comprised 145 volumes and weighed almost 700 pounds. A project such as this took a great amount of time, but it certainly was worth the effort. You will soon have the opportunity to use the international language of the blind as you write a letter to a friend in the Braille alphabet.

A Bit Of Braille

A Bit Of Braille

THE BRAILLE PLAN: Although the dots must be raised in order for a blind person to read them, you can still practice the alphabet by using this guide to write your message. Braille got the idea for his alphabet from a French army captain who used a similar code to send messages to his soldiers at night. Close your eyes for a few minutes and listen to the sounds around you. Then, using the Braille alphabet below, write a message to a friend, describing what you heard. You might also want to describe what you felt and smelled as well.

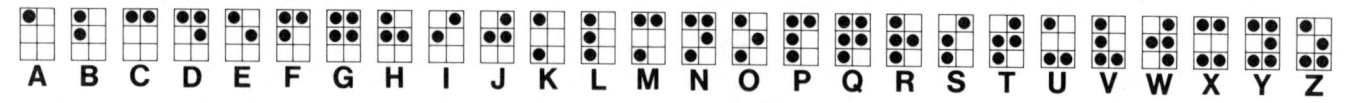

A B C D E F G H I J K L M N O P Q R S T U V W X Y Z

Write your message here:

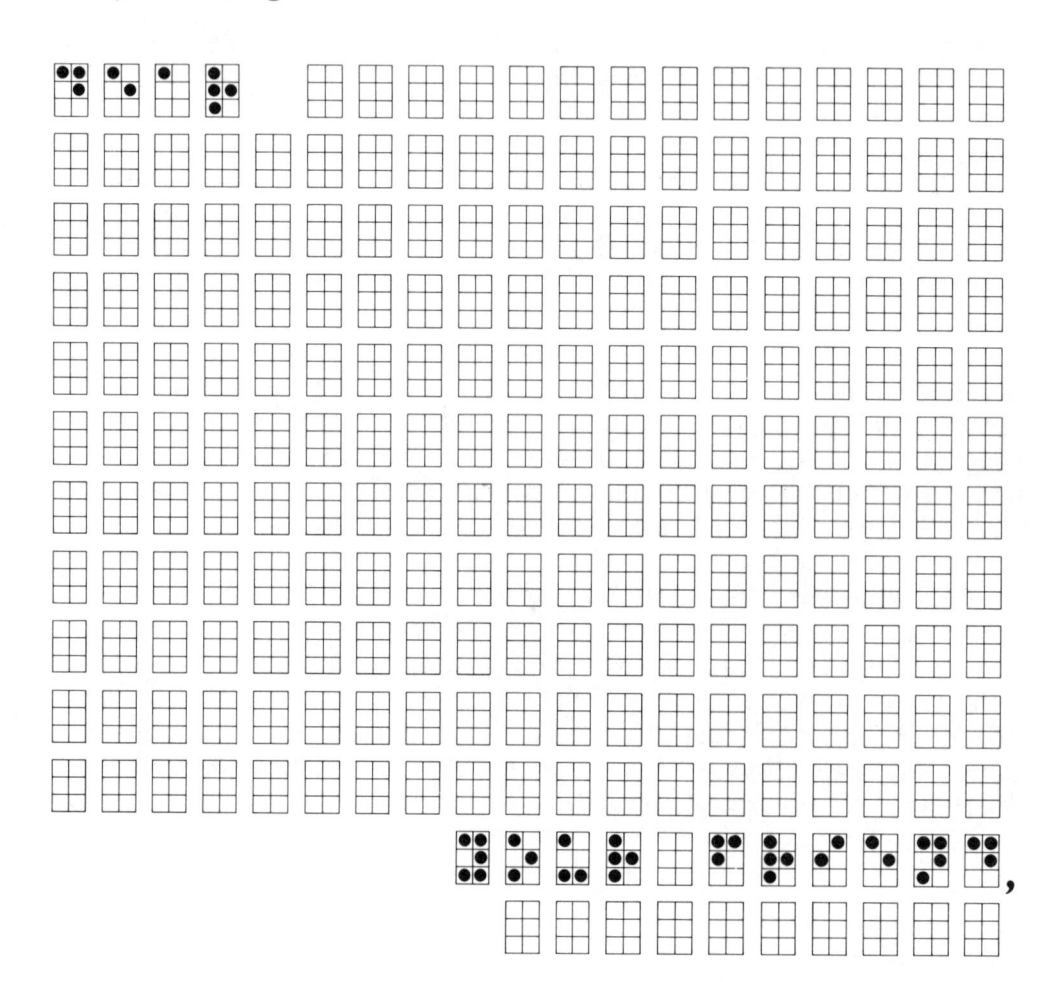

January

February

Tune Up Your Teeth

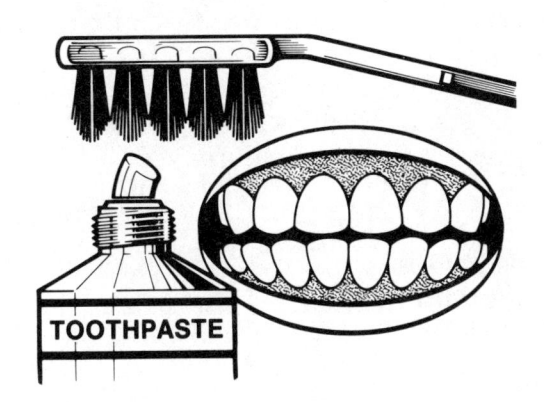

What could the Emperor of the Chinese Chou Dynasty of 700 B.C. have in common with President George Washington's dentist?

The answer to this strange question is particularly important in February as we observe National Children's Dental Health Month. Ancient Chinese artists, working for the Emperor, used a material called porcelain to fashion some of the most beautiful art pieces the world has ever seen. Thousands of years later, George Washington's dentist used porcelain to fashion a set of artificial teeth. This was the first time anyone had been able to make false teeth that were strong enough to withstand the harsh treatment people inflict on their teeth.

Our natural teeth are jacketed in a material that is just as attractive and as strong as porcelain. Called "enamel," this protective jacket is made of the strongest material produced in the human body. But, like any other part of our bodies, this enamel can be severely damaged if not cared for properly.

The food we eat, the beverages we drink, and even the air we breathe can damage the enamel covering our teeth. Regular brushing with a good toothbrush and the use of dental floss after eating can help keep teeth and gums healthy. But brushing and flossing make up just one part of a positive dental health plan. Avoiding those foods like candy and colas that can gradually damage the teeth and gums is important, too. So spread the word! Keep the world smiling as you join in observing National Children's Dental Health Month by creating posters for the cafeteria.

Tune Up Your Teeth

Name _____

Tune Up Your Teeth

HOW TO MAKE THE PERFECT POSTER: In order for any poster to be effective, it must immediately capture the reader's attention. That's why posters often feature bright colors, interesting drawings, and catchy jingles. A jingle is a short attention-grabbing rhyme. Most jingles are designed to convince the reader to do something, such as brush teeth more often. Read the following jingle, and then write some of your own for the subjects listed below. When you've finished, use your favorite jingle on your poster.

> Poor Jeremy Jonathan Heath,
> Would never brush his teeth.
> Now he has a cavity
> about the size of Cincinnati.

WRITE A JINGLE ABOUT THE NEED FOR BRUSHING:

_____
_____
_____

WRITE A JINGLE ABOUT THE NEED TO USE DENTAL FLOSS EVERY DAY:

_____
_____
_____

WRITE A JINGLE ABOUT EATING THE RIGHT KINDS OF FOODS:

_____
_____
_____

February

February

Bright Ideas Can Light Up Your Life

How long would it take you to memorize the names of the inventors of wax paper, the movie projector, synthetic rubber, the phonograph, and the electric light?

One man, known as "the wizard of Menlo Park," invented these and more than twenty other products that we take for granted today. Thomas Alva Edison, the world's greatest inventor, was born on February 11, 1847. By the time he was ten years old, Edison had begun to show a great interest in improving life through his genius for creating new things.

He was just twenty years old when he patented his first invention. At the time, Thomas Edison was working as a telegrapher for an eastern railroad. During his free time, he built a machine which could automatically record votes during an election. Edison's vote-counting machine is still used today in some states, although the patent has long since expired.

The patents Edison received protected his inventions from being duplicated and sold by someone else without Edison's permission. A patent is a U.S. Government document that guarantees the inventor the exclusive right to his idea for seventeen years. After that time, the idea becomes available to anyone who wishes to copy it.

Each year, the United States Trademark and Patent Office sponsors National Inventor's Day. On February 9 and 10, inventors from all across the country travel to Washington, D.C. to meet with one another and demonstrate their new ideas. On the afternoon of the tenth, they hold a meeting to induct new members into the Inventors Hall of Fame.

Perhaps you will have the opportunity to enter the Hall of Fame after you complete your first sample patent application.

Bright Ideas Can Light Up Your Life

Name _____

Bright Ideas Can Light Up Your Life

INVENTOR'S INSTRUCTIONS: Have you ever seen a machine that can: • walk a dog? • make your bed? • get you home from school in seconds? Think of a machine that would make your life easier. Make a complete drawing of your invention, identifying each important part, and then describe your invention using as much detail as possible. Explain how it will improve the quality of life, how it can be used, and why you feel your invention should be granted a patent.

USE THIS SPACE TO SKETCH YOUR INVENTION:

USE THIS SPACE TO EXPLAIN YOUR INVENTION (use additional paper to complete the description):

_____
_____
_____
_____
_____

February

February

Be A Weather Wizard

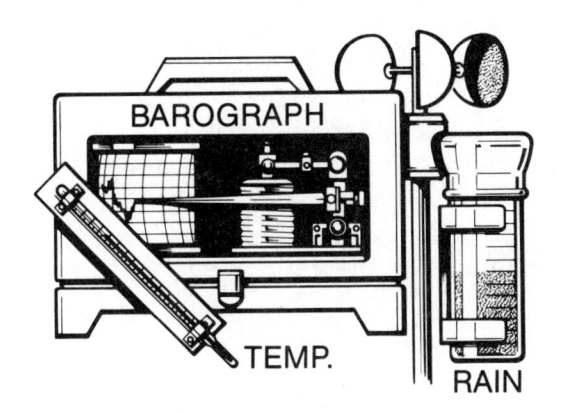

Why might the fiddler crab and the elk be good pets for a weather forecaster to have?

Scientists have discovered that the way some animals act can signal a change in the weather. Elks crowd under large trees two days before heavy snows arrive. Fiddler crabs often dig secure shelters before hurricanes. Some people believe the number of rings on the woolly caterpillar can tell us whether we face a harsh winter. Fortunately, forecasters now have far more sophisticated means of predicting the weather.

Today, the local weather forecaster you see each evening on television has a variety of instruments and machines to help predict tomorrow's weather. Computers, high-altitude radar, and satellite photographs give the forecaster a fairly good idea of the type of weather traveling toward a particular area. But the forecaster also uses instruments that have been available for years. Thermometers, wind meters, barometers, and rain gauges collect information about the weather currently surrounding an area. In addition, the National Weather Service provides the forecaster with information the United States Government has gathered for the region. It takes an experienced forecaster about two and a half hours to collect all of the information needed to make a three-minute television report.

Much of the information the television weather forecaster collects is also available to you. Check your local newspaper for the national weather summary. It most likely lists the high and low temperatures, wind speeds, and precipitation for the last twenty-four hours. Forecasters all across the country help write these summaries. Join with them in celebrating National Weather Forecaster's Day on February 5. On the next page you will have the opportunity to do a bit of forecasting of your own.

Be A Weather Wizard

Name _____

Be A Weather Wizard

PROGNOSTICATION POSSIBILITIES: Weather forecasters are also called "prognosticators" because they predict what the weather will be in the future based on what they know now. You can do the same thing with some easily obtained information. The guide below will help you compile all of the data you need to make a weather forecast. When you have all of the information you want, write a three-minute weather program similar to those you see on your local television stations.

WEATHER WORD

Date _____ Time _____

High temperature in town yesterday _____

Low temperature in town today _____

Wind direction _____

Wind speed _____

Sky conditions (cloudy, clear, etc.) _____

Amount of precipitation _____

Are there any storms in neighboring states that might blow into your area? _____

What has the weather been like for the last few days in your area?

_____

_____

Is the current temperature closer to yesterday's high or yesterday's low?

_____

Has the temperature been rising or falling over the last few days?

_____

Begin writing your weather broadcast on this form and use additional paper as needed. You might want to write your final forecast on note cards since they are easier to hold when speaking.

_____

_____

February

February

Music With Morse

TELEGRAPH KEY

•••• •— •—•• •—•• —•—•   —••• •• •—• — •••• —•• •— —••—

If not for the genius of Samuel Morse, this message might never have reached its destination. Morse invented the first effective telegraph system in 1840. Later, he introduced a system of dots and dashes to transmit messages over long-distance telegraph lines. Using Morse Code and a sensitive electrical switch called a key, a telegraph operator could send messages across the country. The operator at the other end of the line could then translate the dots and dashes back into understandable sentences.

Morse foresaw many uses for his great invention, but the Postal Cable Telegraph Company's plan surely would have surprised and amused him. On February 10, 1933, the New York office of the company delivered the first singing telegram. Soon this service was being offered all across the country. Sending birthday greetings, anniversary wishes, and holiday messages in song became very popular. The service lasted several years before it was discontinued.

As more and more people installed telephones in their homes, the popularity of the telegram dropped. But recently, several small companies have begun once again to deliver singing messages. The larger telegraph companies, seeing the rising popularity of this service, are reviving it in selected parts of the country.

Don't feel left out if the service hasn't yet reached your home town. On the next page you are going to have the chance to write a singing telegram of your own! And for those who don't know Morse Code, the message above says "Happy Birthday."

Music With Morse

Name _____

Music With Morse

MEMO TO MUSICIANS: Music has always been an important part of life. Ancient warriors used music to announce the beginning and the end of battles. Sheep herders in Europe used music to talk to one another as they sat on hillsides guarding their flocks. Today, we often use melodies and lyrics to send happy messages to one another. Using the commonly recognized melodies mentioned below, write an appropriate message for each occasion.

Using the melody of "Happy Birthday to You," write a birthday message to a friend.

_____
_____
_____
_____
_____
_____

Using the melody of "She'll Be Comin' Round the Mountain," write a telegraphic message to a relative announcing that you will soon be arriving for a long visit.

_____
_____
_____
_____
_____
_____

Think of some other melodies that might lend themselves to short, telegraphic messages.

February

February

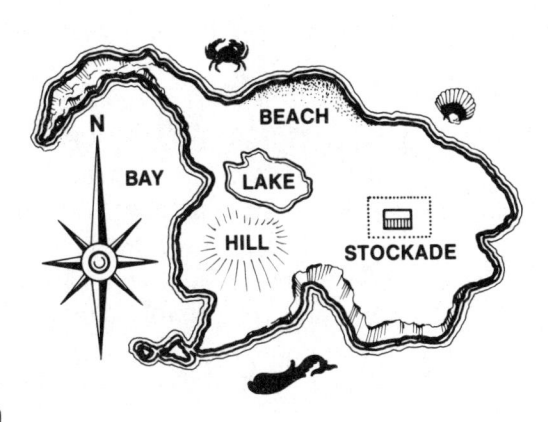

Most Dangerous Mission

When Daniel DeFoe wrote the popular story, *Robinson Crusoe*, few people were aware that the story was almost as much fact as it was fiction. DeFoe's work was based on the true adventures of a Scottish sailor named Alexander Selkirk.

In the book, DeFoe tells the story of a sailor marooned on an island in the South Sea. Crusoe survives on the island by learning to live off the land. He learns how to use fallen trees to build a house, how to tame wild animals, and how to defend himself against attack. After several years of living alone, Crusoe rescues a man being held by a cannibalistic tribe. Crusoe names the man "Friday" in recognition of the day of the rescue. The two remain together, and Friday becomes Crusoe's servant and friend. After twenty-eight years on the island, Crusoe makes contact with a ship and, with Friday, returns to England.

The real story of Alexander Selkirk is not nearly as exciting as DeFoe's tale. The Scottish sailor signed on with a pirate expedition in the early 1700's and began sailing the Caribbean. After he argued with the captain of his ship, Selkirk demanded to be put ashore on the nearest island. The captain agreed to the strange request, and Selkirk took refuge on a small island 400 miles west of the coast of Chile. He lived alone on the island for almost four and a half years until he was finally rescued by a passing ship on February 12, 1709.

Think for a moment how you would feel if you lived in the days of Alexander Selkirk and suddenly found yourself living alone on a desert island.

Most Dangerous Mission

A STORYTELLER'S STYLE: One of the reasons DeFoe's book was so popular was that it was written in a narrative style. A narrative style is one that tells a story from a particular viewpoint. The story below is told from the viewpoint of Cliff Hickleson, a captain in Her Majesty's Royal Navy in the early 1700's. Read the beginning of the story, and then write a plausible conclusion in the narrative style.

"It's still hard to know where to begin. These last twenty-four hours have been some of the strangest in my life. Just yesterday morning we received the news that strange ships had been seen floating toward the southern coast. And then yesterday afternoon, just before sunset, we saw the orange-red glare of a ship burning on the horizon.

"We all knew it was foolish to sail full speed at night, but the wind was good and the sails tight. It must have been just before midnight when we reached the wreck. The main sail had snapped — almost as if it had been pulled down. Only the port side of the boat was burned. That was a sure sign that someone had put out the fire. But we searched and found only the dead. Not one of them was burned; not one of them could have put out the fire.

"And then I heard that cold, bone-chilling rumble as the wind came up, tossing my ship against the hull of the wreck. I tried to swing back aboard and drop anchor, but I must have failed. I remember nothing else until waking here on this deserted island. My ship is gone. My men are nowhere to be seen. I don't know what happened to me, but I am all the more convinced that pirates are again trying to take control of the South Seas. I must develop a plan to free myself from this island and stop the pirate lootings.

"First, I will... _____

_____

_____

_____

_____ continue using your own paper.

February

March

Awareness Helps

Q: What does the Woolly Spider Monkey of Brazil have in common with the great Japanese Sea Lion?

The answer to this question, unfortunately, is an unhappy one. Both the spider monkey and the great sea lion are endangered species. These animals, and dozens of others, are dying out — some slowly, others very rapidly. As the world changes and people place new demands on the land, many animal species are unable to adapt to their changing environment. If no one acts to save these creatures, they may one day become extinct, disappearing completely and forever from the face of the Earth.

It is the goal of the National Wildlife Federation to call attention to the difficulties all animals face. Each year, during the third week of March, the Federation sponsors National Wildlife Week. The Federation supplies posters, information packets, and film presentations to schools and community groups. With the assistance of such noted honorary chairpersons as film star Robert Redford, the Federation is helping people change the way they think about the Earth and the animals that inhabit it. When more people are aware of the problem of endangered species, more people can act to protect our environment.

You can join in the effort, too. On the next page you'll find a list of some of the world's endangered species. Use the encyclopedia to find out more about them and what might be done to save these animals from extinction.

Name _____

Awareness Helps

RESEARCH REQUIREMENTS: When gathering information about a particular animal, try to use several different sources. If you were to investigate the life of the Japanese Sea Lion, for example, you could look through an encyclopedia, check the card catalog for any nonfiction books on sea mammals, and ask the librarian about filmstrips or film loops that discuss sea lions. Select one of the animals listed below, and locate the requested information. Then write a short essay in which you state your ideas about how people might work to save the endangered species from extinction.

SOME ENDANGERED SPECIES: Mexican grizzly bear, northern swift fox, golden lion marmoset, woolly spider monkey, giant otter, Novaya Zemlya reindeer, several species of rhinoceros, several species of seal, blue whale, red wolf.

NAME OF ANIMAL _____

WHERE COMMONLY FOUND _____

APPROXIMATELY HOW MANY STILL IN EXISTENCE? _____

REASONS FOR THEIR DECLINE _____

_____

_____

_____

WHAT DO YOU FEEL CAN BE DONE TO REVERSE THE

PROBLEM AND SAVE THE SPECIES? _____

_____

_____

_____

_____ USE AN ADDITIONAL SHEET OF PAPER.

March

March

Solla Sollew To You

How do you feel about green eggs and ham?
What's the shortest route to Solla Sollew?
Is it possible to move a northbound Zax?

The answers to these questions can't be found in a cookbook or on a map. An encyclopedia won't help much either. Only an expert knows the correct answers to these questions. Fortunately, there are millions of experts — young children around the world who enjoy the many zany characters of Dr. Seuss.

Born March 2, 1904, Theodor Seuss Geisel began his career as an illustrator and humorist. He published the classic *To Think I Saw it on Mulberry Street* in 1937. Since that time Dr. Seuss has gone on to write dozens of other colorfully illustrated and humorously entertaining stories. In fact, several of his more popular stories have recently been made into animated TV specials.

Much of Dr. Seuss' popularity is due to his storytelling style. Using a carefully prepared rhythm and cleverly rhyming words, Dr. Seuss can create an interesting story without using words that are too difficult for a young reader. Listen to the rhythm as you read the closing sentences of Dr. Seuss' *The Zax*.

> Of course the world didn't stand still.
> The world grew.
> In a couple of years, the new highway came through
> and they built it right over those two stubborn Zax.
> And left them there, standing unbudged in their tracks.

Now we know that you can't budge a Zax. But you can take a pencil and paper and facts...and write your own story about a town made of wax.

Solla Sollew To You

Solla Sollew To You

PICTURE BOOK POINTERS: When writing stories for young children, it is important to use short, easy-to-understand sentences. Rhyming words often can capture the imagination of the young listener. Another way to interest the listener in the story is to illustrate it with colorful and interesting pictures. Since the pictures will take up most of the page, you will need several sheets of paper for this assignment. Think of a small town made entirely of wax. What might it look like? What kind of people would live in such a town? What kinds of jobs might they have? What would they do for recreation? What adventures (and misadventures) might the residents of the town have? The answers to all of these questions lie in your imagination. Think about them for a short time and then begin writing and illustrating your story. When you finish, share it with some students in school who are still too young to read.

(BEGIN YOUR STORY HERE) _____

_____

_____

March

March

Heads Up!

Here is a short multiple-choice test:

There are more people living in New York City than in:
A. Alaska
B. New Mexico
C. Hawaii
D. All of the above

It may be hard to believe, but the correct answer to this short test is "D." More than seven million people live in New York City. According to the U.S. Government's most recent figures, the combined population of Alaska, New Mexico, and Hawaii is just under three million people.

The Government has always been interested in knowing how many people reside in the country. As early as 1790 the Congress recognized that proper representation depended on correctly counting the number of U.S citizens. On March 1, 1790, Congress ordered the first official census — or count — of the population. A few months later, seventeen federal marshals and six hundred citizens counted all 3,939,326 residents of the United States.

Since that first count, the Government has conducted a census every decade. During each year ending in "0," the U.S. Census Bureau attempts to count everyone residing within the borders of the United States. This includes people living alone high up in the mountains as well as those in small communities on the desert floor. It's not easy to complete a census for a big country like the United States of America.

Today, instead of using federal marshals to count each citizen, the Census Bureau relies on the mail. During the last census, the Bureau mailed more than 75 million questionnaires to addresses across the country. The Government also hired census takers to interview difficult-to-contact residents. On the next page you'll discover the fun of acting as a census taker in your school.

Heads Up!

Name _____

Heads Up!

ENUMERATOR'S EXPLANATION: A person who records information for an official census is called an enumerator. An enumerator is responsible for correctly counting everyone in a given area. This information is then turned over to other enumerators who write a summary of the information, drawing conclusions about where people live. Pick a particular group in your school to enumerate. Then, using the information you receive by asking the questions below, write a short summary describing the group you interview. There are three open spaces in this interview form. Use them to write your own questions.

The Heads Up Census
(You will need one form for each person you interview)

(1) Age _____ (2) Grade in school _____

(3a) List the ages of any brothers in family _____

(3b) List the ages of any sisters in family _____

(4a) Any pets in the household?   ☐ yes   ☐ no

(4b) What kind of pet(s)? _____

(5a) Any radios in the household?   ☐ yes   ☐ no

(5b) How many? _____

(5c) Any televisions in the household?   ☐ yes   ☐ no

(5d) How many? _____

(6) What are this person's favorite free-time activities?

_____   _____   _____

(7) _____

(8) _____

(9) _____

Use your findings to write an accurate summary on another piece of paper. Discuss how many people have brothers and sisters in their families, what most of the people interviewed like to do for fun, and so forth.

March

March

Adopt An Artist

Do you know...

who is remembered as both a talented painter and the inventor of the telegraph?

who completed 1,500 paintings in her lifetime even though she didn't begin her artistic career until her seventy-fifth birthday?

how many times the Mona Lisa was actually painted before the artist was satisfied with his portrait?

Artists of the world, take a bow! For more than twenty years, March has been officially recognized as Youth Art Month. This seems appropriate since several great artists — including Vincent Van Gogh and Michelangelo — were born during the month.

Youthful artists have created some of the world's greatest masterpieces. Michelangelo, a painter, sculptor, and architect, was only twelve years old when he began working as an apprentice artist in Florence, Italy. Rembrandt, one of the world's most honored artists, began painting while still quite young.

Spend some time in the library looking through books about artists (most of these books can be found with Dewey Decimal call numbers between 700 and 799). Look for examples of well-known artists who began their successful careers while still in their youth. On the next page, you will receive instructions on how to write a short biography of that person.

Samuel Morse (see February) was a famous painter as well as the inventor of the telegraph. Anna Mary Robertson Moses, remembered as Grandma Moses, completed 1,500 paintings during her short career. What we see as the Mona Lisa is actually painted over three other portraits of Senora Giaconda, the subject of the portrait.

Adopt An Artist

Name _____

ADOPT AN ARTIST

BLUEPRINT FOR A BIOGRAPHY: One of the best ways to learn about someone who lived before your time is to read a history of the person. This type of personal history is called a biography. To write a biography, the author must first learn everything he can about his subject. This often means reading about the person in other biographies, magazines, and encyclopedias. The outline below is designed to help you get started on your biography of an artist. Find the answers to these questions, and then use what you've learned to write the biography. You may want to draw a picture of the artist and display both the picture and the biography in the school library or art room.

ARTIST'S NAME _____

DATE OF BIRTH _____

PLACE OF BIRTH _____

HOW MANY PEOPLE IN FAMILY? _____

BRIEFLY DESCRIBE EARLY CHILDHOOD OF THE ARTIST _____

_____

_____

WHEN DID THE ARTIST BEGIN CAREER? _____

_____

WHERE DID THE ARTIST LIVE DURING PROFESSIONAL CAREER? _____

WHAT MEDIUM DID THE ARTIST USE? (sculpture, painting, pottery)

_____

WHAT WAS THE ARTIST'S FIRST SUCCESSFUL WORK? _____

_____

DID THE ARTIST CONTINUE CAREER THROUGH ENTIRE LIFE? _____

WHEN DID THE ARTIST DIE? _____

Use the answers to these questions to guide you through the writing of the biography. Use as much paper as necessary.

March

March

How To Say NO!

Years after he invented the telephone, Alexander Graham Bell was occasionally disturbed by unwanted telephone calls from people trying to sell him something.

Certainly Bell wasn't disturbed by his telephone message of March 10, 1876. While preparing for a test of his unproven telephone system, Bell accidentally spilled battery acid over some equipment. Trying to mop up the mess, he said, "Come here Watson. I need you."

Thomas Watson, Bell's assistant, was upstairs at the time setting up a second telephone. Imagine his surprise when he heard Bell's voice clearly through the telephone receiver. This accident turned out to be the first successful test of the telephone. In just a few years, the popularity of Bell's invention had spread around the globe.

Today, the telephone continues to be the most important communication tool in the world. In Washington, D.C., where Bell once lived and worked, there are now more telephones than people. Worldwide, the more than 300 million phones range from Australia to scientific research stations on the North Pole. Each day, people use these phones to make and receive millions of calls.

Unfortunately, not all telephone calls are necessary or welcome. Selling merchandise and services by telephone continues to grow more common each year. Today, computers can be programmed to dial a number automatically, play a recorded message, and even take orders for merchandise. But you don't have to listen to unwanted calls. There are ways to say no and mean it. So find a partner and start practicing.

How To Say NO!

Name _____

How To Say NO!

TELEPHONE TIPS: A telephone conversation is actually a dialogue between two people. Whenever you get tired of listening to someone talk to you on the telephone, you should be able to end the conversation — politely, but firmly. Some telephone sales people, however, are quite persistent. They know that the longer they keep you on the phone, the more likely you are to buy something just to get rid of them. The beginning of a telephone sales speech is presented below. Have your partner take the role of the telephone solicitor and you play yourself. The solicitor will write the part of the dialogue designed to keep you on the phone. You will write your own part of the dialogue, trying to get rid of the unwanted caller. If you want to know more about this subject, write a letter to your local Bell telephone office and ask for a copy of the booklet "What To Do About Annoying Telephone Calls."

Telephone Solicitor: Good afternoon, my name is Harry Klabbitt. I am with the Acme Reading Book Company...

You: Hello, Mr. Klabbitt. Listen, I'm terribly busy right now.

Telephone Solicitor: Of course you're busy. That's why you need to subscribe to the Acme Company's great new plan. For just twelve dollars a week, you can get ten exciting books written by unknown authors.

You: I don't have to buy your books. I can get all of the books I want from the public library.

Using these lines and additional paper, continue this dialogue until you have fully discussed the books, the price, why you don't want them, and why you don't have time to listen to his speech. Try to write a surprising conclusion.

_____
_____
_____
_____
_____
_____
_____ CONTINUE ON YOUR OWN PAPER.

March

April
The Responsible Rider's Test

TRUE OR FALSE: Anyone using the streets must be able to identify the meaning of each of these signs.

Surprisingly, the answer to this question is false. While automobile drivers must pass a test which calls for them to identify these signs before receiving a license, few states give a similar test to bicycle riders.

The number of bicycle riders on U.S. streets and highways has increased dramatically since April 22, 1884. On that date, Thomas Stevens of California set out from San Francisco for the first bicycle trip around the world. It took more than two years for him to complete the entire trip. Stevens arrived back in San Francisco early in 1887 aboard a freighter from Japan.

Imagine how different the trip would be today, a century later. In addition to riding through strange lands, a round-the-world cyclist would face thousands of busy intersections, flashing traffic signals, and cars that zip down expressways at high speeds.

Because byicicle riders do face so many dangers today, local Optimist Clubs — in cooperation with police departments and schools — sponsor Bicycle Safety Week during the third week of April. During the week volunteers make free bicycle inspections, promote safe riding skills, and conduct a bicycle rodeo. Bicycle Safety Week aims at helping everyone become a better cyclist and remember the rules of the road.

One way to find out just how much people know about bicycle safety rules is to give a test. You will have the opportunity to do exactly that after you write a test of your own.

The Responsible Rider's Test

Name _____

The Responsible Rider's Test

TESTING TIPS: Tests can ask several kinds of questions. Perhaps the most common are the true-false, multiple choice, and the matching. These are all called closed questions. That means there are just a few answers the person who is taking the test can choose. Short answer or essay questions, in contrast, are open questions. After studying the examples of both kinds of questions below, write three of each type of closed question and two open questions. When you're finished, exchange your test with other people in your class. They can take your test, and you can try theirs. Good Luck!

EXAMPLES:

TRUE-FALSE: All bicycle tires must be filled with 85 pounds of air pressure.

MULTIPLE CHOICE: The part of the bike which holds the front wheel is the
   A. saddle   B. fork   C. spokes

MATCHING:
1. chain — A. the part of the bike that holds the pedals
2. reflector — B. the object that shines when struck by light
3. crank — C. the part of the bike that moves the wheel

ESSAY QUESTION: What would you do if your brake cable broke while you were speeding downhill?

Using another sheet of paper, write your own test that includes these four parts:

THE RESPONSIBLE RIDER'S TEST

PART ONE: TRUE-FALSE

PART TWO: MULTIPLE CHOICE

PART THREE: MATCHING

PART FOUR: SHORT ANSWER/ESSAY QUESTIONS

April

April

The North Pole Is Missing!

Where in the world could you go to get a long night's sleep?

One place you might want to try is the North Pole. In darkness for half of each year, the North Pole remains one of the most secluded spots on the globe. It wasn't until April 6, 1909, after more than twenty years of trying, that the first explorers finally reached the North geographic Pole.

For many years, Admiral Robert Peary had been attempting to be the first person to reach the North Pole. He'd made several other trips before finally achieving his goal in April 1909. During one of his earliest trips, Peary had reached the outer edge of the polar ice caps. On other trips he had found samples of large meteorites that had crashed into the top of the world. When he finally reached the North Pole, Peary wrote in his diary, "It all seems so simple and commonplace." It was hard for him to believe he'd finally achieved his goal after so many years of trying.

Another icy first also took place on April 6, but a few years before Peary reached the Pole. Nicholas H. Borgfeldt, an American inventor, was granted a patent for the "Borgfeldt Snow Melting Apparatus." By collecting snow and then pressing it against a heated surface, Borgfeldt's invention was supposed to clear snow-covered sidewalks in minutes. Unfortunately, Borgfeldt's idea never really caught on.

What do you suppose would have happened if Admiral Peary had taken a "Borgfeldt Snow Melting Apparatus" with him on his North Pole expedition? Don't think too long because in a moment you will have the opportunity to write, "The North Pole is Missing!"

The North Pole Is Missing!

The North Pole Is Missing!

FACT AND FICTION: Science fiction is another popular form of writing. Although much of the story comes from the imagination of the writer, some revolves around actual scientific discoveries. In "The North Pole Is Missing!" Gar Raider, the hero of the story, must stop the evil Dr. Chell from melting the North Pole and flooding New York. Read the beginning passages of the story, and then write your own spellbinding conclusion.

Gar was sitting in his office near the White House when the call came in.

"It's the President," Gar's secretary said. "He wants to see you right away. Frankly, I thought he sounded worried."

Climbing into his solar-powered sports car, Gar set the controls for 1600 Pennsylvania Avenue, the address of the White House. Within seconds he waved to the guard as he stopped near the President's oval office.

Gar's secretary had been right. The President was worried. He handed Gar a small blue piece of paper as the detective entered the office.

"It's from Dr. Chell," the President explained, dropping into the dark red leather chair behind his desk. "I am afraid it means trouble."

"I thought the doctor was living on the North Pole," Gar said as he began to read the note. "How much trouble can he cause up there?"

"Plenty, I'm afraid," the President responded. "According to that note, Dr. Chell will use his latest invention to melt the entire North Pole unless we pay him three trillion dollars by noon tomorrow."

Gar nodded and then looked at his watch. "That gives me just over twenty-four hours to stop him," he said. "I think I have a plan."

The President smiled for the first time that day. "I was hoping you would say that, Gar. Tell me what you plan to do."

April

April

The Stranger Exchange

"Neither sleet, nor rain, nor dark of night shall keep us from our appointed rounds."

The young riders of the Pony Express certainly took the unofficial motto of the United States Postal Service to heart as they began regular operations on April 2, 1860. Determined to get the mail from Missouri to California faster than it could be delivered by stage coach, the express riders rode day and night in every kind of weather.

During the winter months, the riders carried the mail over snow-packed Rocky Mountain passes and then through the flat, desolate stretches of Utah. Each rider would travel about seventy-five miles, stopping only to change horses. Because saving time was very important, many riders could change horses and be back on the trail in under a minute. At the end of his assigned trip, the rider would hand the bags to a waiting rider on a fresh horse. If a new rider wasn't ready to take over, the tired expressman would have to continue west until he reached the next station. For this bone-breaking work, a Pony Express rider received about $125 a month. And in less than two years, the riders were looking for new jobs as the Pony Express went out of business.

Seventy-five years later, letter sending took another giant step forward. On April 19, 1937, a letter mailed in New York became the first piece of mail to circle the globe. It first went to San Francisco, and then to Hong Kong, Penang, Amsterdam, and Brazil. Thirty-six days later the letter arrived back in New York.

Today, it's possible for a letter mailed on Monday to arrive the next day on the other side of the American continent or even in some foreign country. You will have a chance to prove this possibility yourself as you enter the Stranger Exchange.

The Stranger Exchange

Name _____

The Stranger Exchange

THE PEN PAL PLAN: If you have a friend who lives far from you, you already know that communicating by mail is quite inexpensive and effective. You also know the fun of receiving mail from someone living far away. If you don't know someone living in a distant city, you and your classmates can find pen pals there. Pick a city you'd like to know more about, and have your teacher put all of the letters in a large envelope addressed to the school district offices in the city you picked. The district offices can then forward your letters to a school similar to yours. On this page you'll find an outline for a friendly letter. Write a rough draft of your letter here, and then copy it on a clean sheet of paper.

_____
(today's date)

_____
(your street address)

_____
(city, state, zip code)

Dear Friend, _____
(the greeting)

_____

_____

_____

_____

       Sincerely,
       (the closing)

       (your signature)

April

April

Newsview: The Five O'Clock Report

Listen, my children, and you shall hear
Of the midnight ride of Paul Revere...

On the evening of April 18, 1775, Paul Revere — a Boston silversmith — learned of a British plan to punish American colonists who objected to the way England was treating them. General Thomas Gage, the commander of the British soldiers, was told to march into the Massachusetts towns of Lexington and Concord. The plan was to capture the Americans' supply of gunpowder and rifles, and arrest the patriots — the name taken by the freedom-seeking colonists.

Paul Revere knew he had to warn his friends. Since there was no radio or television and no time to publish the British plan in the newspapers, Revere set out from Boston on a borrowed horse. He arrived in Lexington around midnight and headed straight for the patriot headquarters at the home of the Reverend Mr. Clark. Paul Revere knew that two of the patriot leaders, John Hancock and Samuel Adams, would be there. But since the Reverend Clark didn't know Paul Revere, he almost refused to let the Boston silversmith inside. If Hancock had not heard Paul Revere's voice at the door, the message might never have been delivered. But he did, and the patriots were ready for the British when the troops marched into town.

Revere continued on toward Concord, but he was arrested by another group of British soldiers before he could finish his famous ride. Today, an entire nation can receive emergency information in an instant over radio and television. What do you suppose Paul Revere's message of 1775 might have sounded like if announced on a national news broadcast? You will soon have a chance to find out as you produce the evening news.

Newsview: The Five O'Clock Report

Newsview: The Five O'Clock Report

Name _____

REPORTER'S REQUIREMENTS: A good news report should contain five important elements: who, what, where, when, and why. Use the encyclopedia and any books you have on the American Revolution to learn more about Paul Revere and his famous ride. After you have collected all of the information you need, write a two-minute news report detailing the information you found. Think of other news reports you've heard as you begin to write your own. The outline below will help you organize your information for your report.

WHO IS THE IMPORTANT PERSON IN THIS REPORT? _____
_____

    WHAT IS HIS OCCUPATION? _____

    WHERE DOES HE LIVE? _____

WHAT DID HE DO THAT WAS NEWSWORTHY? _____
_____

    HOW DID HE DO IT? _____
_____

WHERE DID THIS ACTIVITY TAKE PLACE? _____

    DID HE ACT ALONE, OR DID HE HAVE HELP? _____
_____

WHEN DID HE DO HIS NEWSWORTHY ACT? _____

WHY DID HE DO IT? _____
_____

WHAT OTHER PEOPLE WERE INVOLVED IN THIS ACTIVITY?

(list any friends, associates, and enemies) _____
_____

LIST ANY OTHER IMPORTANT INFORMATION YOU CAN USE

IN YOUR BROADCAST. _____
_____

Now write your story on another sheet of paper using this outline as your guide.

April

April

THE PERSONAL PRIZE

Who says prizes are just for kids?

Joseph Pulitzer, one of America's greatest newspaper editors, certainly didn't think so. In his will, Pulitzer left two million dollars of his savings to Columbia University. Part of the money was to be used to start a new School of Journalism at the University. The rest was to be awarded to writers of exceptional newspaper articles, books, and other works of literary merit.

Today, the Pulitzer Prize is one of the most prestigious awards a writer can receive. Each year, newspapers all across the country mail entries to the Pulitzer Prize committee at Columbia University. Journalists from throughout the United States serve as judges for the competition. After the judges make their decision, the prizes are awarded during the first week in April — in honor of Pulitzer's birthday on April 10, 1847.

In addition to receiving a certificate of award, each Pulitzer Prize winner receives a cash prize of $1,000. But it is the honor more than the cash that most Pulitzer Prize winners treasure. It often takes years of training and dedication before a journalist has the skills necessary to win a Pulitzer Prize.

You can do today what Joseph Pulitzer did more than fifty years ago. Start your own awards program. But before you make your first presentation, you will have to decide what it takes to make a great story.

The Personal Prize

Name _____

THE PERSONAL PRIZE

A CREATIVE COMPETITION: During the year you have developed skills in several different areas of writing. Select one of your assignments and enter it in a writing competition. In the meantime, design a prize certificate of your own that you can present to the author of a piece you think is outstanding. Remember that before you can award a prize, you must first establish the reasons why that particular entry is worthy of the award. These reasons are called "criteria." The outline below will help you establish the criteria for awarding your personal prize. After you've decided on a winning entry, present your certificate of award to the author.

What kind of writing do you want to honor?
- ☐ mystery fiction ☐ adventure fiction ☐ science fiction
- ☐ other (please describe) _____

Are illustrations necessary for a particular writing entry to win your

personal prize? If so, what kind of illustrations? _____

_____

_____

What criteria do you use to judge an entry? In other words, what are the reasons for choosing a particular entry to win your personal prize?

1. _____

_____

2. _____

_____

3. _____

_____

4. _____

_____

5. _____

_____

The winner of this personal prize is the entry titled, _____

_____

April

May

"*Elementary, My Dear Watson*"

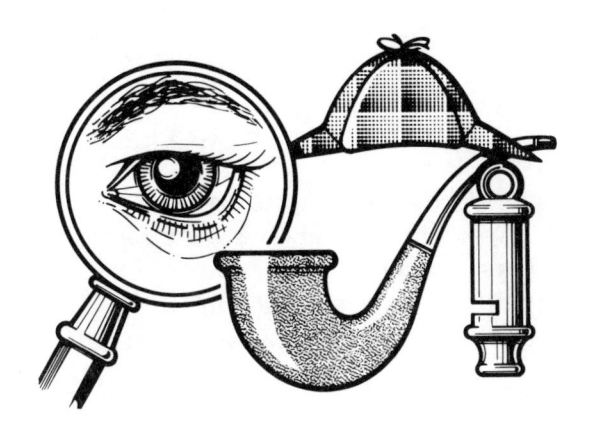

Will the real Sherlock Holmes please stand up?

Sherlock Holmes is the best-known fictional detective in the world. The British sleuth has been featured in dozens of movies, books, and comics.

Sir Arthur Conan Doyle — the creator of Sherlock Holmes — was born on May 22, 1859, and his birthday is celebrated by mystery readers around the world. Surprisingly, Doyle did not intend to become a writer. After graduation from college, Doyle studied medicine. No one will ever know, however, whether the great writer would have become a great doctor. After opening his practice in 1880, Dr. Doyle sat in his office waiting for patients that never came. But instead of wasting his time, he began writing. The first Holmes story, "A Study in Scarlet," was published in 1887, and after that Dr. Doyle gave up medicine to devote all his time to writing.

Mystery readers loved the Holmes stories, and they flooded Doyle with angry mail after the author wrote an 1893 tale in which Sherlock Holmes was killed. Doyle's readers would not allow Holmes to die. Miraculously, Holmes came back to life in Doyle's next book.

Sherlock Holmes' adventures were always filled with odd situations. But Sir Arthur Conan Doyle never resorted to unexplainable tricks or spectacular equipment. With the help of blustery assistant Dr. Watson, Sherlock Holmes solved his cases using wit and logic. You'll need all of your logic, too, because you must now solve "The Case of the Swinging Door."

"Elementary, My Dear Watson"

Name _____

"*Elementary, My Dear Watson*"

SLEUTH'S SOLUTIONS: Try thinking of a mystery story as a series of long and complicated — but interesting — questions. The author of a mystery story can pose several questions in the first chapters and then keep the reader guessing until the last page. The mystery writer's most important task is to make certain that every question gets answered, and that all the answers make sense. You'll find several questions presented in the first paragraphs of "The Case of the Swinging Door." Read the beginning of the story, and then — using your own paper — write an exciting yet logical conclusion to the story.

THE CASE OF THE SWINGING DOOR

A thick fog filled the street. Inspector Phutz-Luce parked his small sports sedan near the corner and waited. He switched off the headlights. The darkness soon closed in around him.

Phutz-Luce waited for almost thirty minutes. He pulled the small slip of paper from the side pocket of his heavy coat. Snapping on a small flashlight, he read the address written in bright green ink. Philbert and Docile Streets. Through the fog, the inspector could see the bright red lights glowing on top of the Docile Tower building. He was in the right place, but where was the messenger?

Suddenly, a pair of headlights flashed on and off three times. Inspector Phutz-Luce slowly climbed from his car and began walking toward the headlights. He would be glad to recover the missing Biltop Diamonds. Just this afternoon, the inspector had received a strange call. The voice on the other end of the line had spoken of stealing the Biltop Diamonds before Phutz-Luce had a chance to pick them up from the special bonded messenger.

Just then, a strange whirring noise filled the air. At first the inspector thought it was the sound of an aircraft, but how could anything fly in this fog? "Bats," he decided to himself. But suddenly, the whirring stopped, and the messenger's car sped away. Why had the messenger suddenly left? When the inspector reached the spot where the car had been parked, all he saw was the door leading to the subway stairway. The door was swinging slowly back and forth. Who could have just come through that door — and where had they gone?

May

May

A Real Estate

ADVERTISEMENT

At Oysterbay on Long Island...there is a very good mill for sale. It has a good brick house with a (smaller) house nearby. It also has a kitchen, workroom (and other rooms)...

Although this advertisement would not attract attention today, it created quite a stir when it first appeared on May 1, 1704. Published in the *Boston News-Letter*, this real estate notice took up less than an inch of space. But it marked the first advertising space ever sold in a newspaper.

The importance of newspaper advertisements has grown tremendously since 1704. Most daily newspapers could not afford to stay in business if they did not sell space for advertisements. Today, more than half of a newspaper is devoted to advertising. The money the paper receives from this advertising is used to pay the reporters, photographers, editors, and others who work for the newspaper. While too many advertisements are an irritation, some are useful.

A well-written advertisement will describe the object or service offered for sale. For example, someone who had read the advertisement above would know something about the property without taking a trip to Oysterbay. But the real estate advertisements you'll find in a newspaper today are much better. Many have a photograph or illustration of the property, and all of them describe the building in detail. Begin thinking of a building you'd like to sell. You are about to become a real estate advertising executive.

A Real Estate

Name _____

A Real Estate

REALTOR'S REVELATIONS: Many real estate agents claim that a good house will sell itself. But nothing gets sold unless buyers know it is for sale. An advertisement tells interested buyers that a property is available, and a good advertisement describes the property using bright and positive words. In addition, the advertisement should help the reader who wants to take a closer look at the property or contact a real estate agent. On this page you'll find some suggestions to help you get your advertisement started. After finishing this page, use your own paper to write the advertisement, and sketch an appropriate illustration of the property.

Type of building offered for sale
☐ school   ☐ office   ☐ home

other _____

Where is the building located? _____

How many stories tall is the building? _____

What material was used to construct the building? _____

How many rooms are in the building? _____

Are the rooms sunny and bright? How many rooms have windows? ____

How much money is the seller asking for building? _____

List all of the interesting parts of the house (special bookcases, large kitchen, gymnasium, etc.) _____

Why would someone want to purchase the building? What could it be used for? Why is this building better than others in the area? _____

May

May

Moms Abound

Let's have three cheers for mothers everywhere!

For centuries, people all around the world have set aside one day a year to honor motherhood. In early England, for example, the day was referred to as Mothering Sunday. It was usually observed in the spring, although no specific date was established. A few small Eastern European countries observed a similar day in late June. In the United States, Mother's Day is always celebrated on the second Sunday in May.

Back in 1872, Julia Howe suggested that June 2 be a day of peace as well as a day to pay respects to our mothers. Her idea spread quickly, and soon there were a number of different Mother's Day observances in different parts of the country.

It was not until 1907 that Anna Jarvis, a public-spirited Philadelphia resident, suggested that the second Sunday in May be the official day of observance for the entire nation. Originally, only two cities — Philadelphia and Grafton, West Virginia — accepted the idea. But in 1914, President Woodrow Wilson signed a resolution proclaiming that date as being Mother's Day throughout the United States.

Today, Mother's Day is observed with all of the fanfare of a major holiday. The observance has grown to include stepmothers, foster mothers, and grandmothers. Americans place more than 20 million long-distance telephone calls during the day, making it one of the busiest for the telephone company. Greeting card sales skyrocket at the beginning of May. In fact, Mother's Day is the second biggest holiday for card manufacturers and stores. But you can relax and avoid the crowds at the checkout counter. On the next page you'll be creating your own Mother's Day card.

Moms Abound

Name _____

Moms Abound

CARD DESIGNER'S DIRECTIVES: A Mother's Day card offers a way of saying "thank-you" to a very special person in your life. Through its message as well as its art, a Mother's Day card can reflect your feelings. This year, why not make a card in the ancient Japanese style of verse known as haiku? Haiku verse has just three lines. The first and last lines contain five syllables each. The second line of verse contains seven syllables. This is an example of a haiku verse:

> Springtime brings the sun.
> Its rays will warm the season
> You still warm my heart.

Write a few haiku verses here. When you've created one that best expresses your thoughts, copy it onto the sheet of plain paper you'll use for your card. For the illustration, you might want to try another Japanese-inspired art form. Place a few drops of colored water on the front of your card. Then, blowing through a straw, move the colored water around the page. It should give you a fascinating and beautiful design. You might want to experiment with scratch paper before painting your card.

Practice haiku verse before deciding on a final verse.

_____
(five syllables)

_____
(seven syllables)

_____
(five syllables)

_____

_____

_____

_____

_____

May

May

ALL ABOARD!

"DONE!"

This one-word telegram told an excited nation that a railway system was complete all the way from the East Coast to California.

On May 10, 1869, at Promontory Point, Utah, a golden spike was driven into the last railroad tie to celebrate the event. Two locomotives — one from the Union Pacific to the east and the other a Central Pacific engine from California — faced each other on a single track. With the completion of the railroad, the young state of California was finally linked by rail to the rest of the nation.

Before long, rail lines and roadways crisscrossed the entire country. Transportation became very important for the growth of the United States. But it wasn't long before an even faster and more efficient transportation system appeared.

On May 2, 1919, Robert Hewitt began the nation's first airline passenger service. The owner and operator of a small airplane, Hewitt flew two women from New York City, New York to Atlantic City, New Jersey. Hewitt's idea quickly spread, and soon airline companies began taking passengers to all parts of the country. Just twenty years later, on May 20, 1939, Pan American World Airlines began regular flights from the United States to Europe.

Today, there are few places on this planet that you can't reach by some form of transportation. Think about where you would like to travel as you become the agent for C.T. World Travel.

All Aboard!

Name _____

ALL ABOARD!

TRAVEL TIPS: Congratulations! You have just been hired as a travel agent by C.T. World Travel. Each year C.T. Travel sponsors an essay contest called, "Why I Want to See America." Your job is to plan a ten-day trip for the winners, taking them any place in the United States. You can use any kind of transportation you wish — bus, train, plane, or car. The plan for such a trip is called an "itinerary." After you finish the itinerary, explain why you selected your ten places to visit. The trip begins July 1 in San Francisco, California and ends there on July 10. Bon voyage!

ITINERARY

Date	Leave	Arrive	Type of Transportation
July 1	San Francisco, CA		
July 2			
July 3			
July 4			
July 5			
July 6			
July 7			
July 8			
July 9			
July 10		San Francisco, CA	airplane

Using these lines, and other paper, write a short description of each place you decided to stop. For example, if you visited Anaheim, California, you would probably want to describe Disneyland. If you visited New York, you might want to describe life in a large city. Wherever you write about, it should sound like an interesting place for a contest winner.

_____

_____

_____

_____

May

May

ALL THE LAW ALLOWS

Scales Of Justice

A TEN-SECOND TEST:

How many new laws are passed in the U.S. each year?
- ☐ about 150 new laws in each state
- ☐ about 50,000 new laws nationwide
- ☐ about 50,000 new laws in each state
- ☐ about 150,000 new laws nationwide

Would you believe that approximately 150,000 laws are passed each year in this country? That's how many the experts think. These new laws become an important part of our society. Without laws, life in America would be much different than it is. In 1958 President Dwight D. Eisenhower recognized the importance of our laws when he proclaimed May 1 as Law Day throughout the country.

Law Day is sponsored by the American Bar Association, a national organization of attorneys. Community groups, schools, and other organizations often put on special Law Day programs. The sponsors of these special programs hope that as people learn more about their laws, they can become better citizens as well.

In addition to Law Day on May 1, the entire first week of May is Respect for Law Week. The purpose of the observance is to honor the law enforcement agencies that work around the clock to protect the rights and property of every citizen in the community. Police officers, fire fighters, lawyers, and judges all work together to keep your community safe.

Not only must all of these people know what the laws of this country are, but they must also know how to carry out the laws with fairness and equality. To do this, most justice officials attend special schools where they review new laws and procedures. You'll soon have a chance to see what these schools might be like as you decide how to use the law.

All The Law Allows

Name _____

ALL THE LAW ALLOWS

A SCHOOL FOR JUDGES: In addition to knowing what the law says, a judge must also know how to apply the law fairly. Sometimes groups of judges hold special meetings during which they pretend to conduct a full trial. Instead of using a real jury and witnesses, however, the judges take turns playing these parts. This is called a "simulation." Read the case below. List all of the arguments that could be made for either side. Then, with the help of two friends, write a script showing how this case might be decided in court. One of you should play the part of the judge, one should play the store owner, and the third person should take the part of the truck driver.

THE CASE OF THE DAMAGED DELIVERY

On October 15, Mr. Bob Walker ordered sixteen cases of bite-size chocolate bars. He wanted to have them on display in his store for Halloween.

The sixteen cases of candy arrived at the Midtown Shipping Terminal on October 31. They were loaded into Harry Verner's delivery truck at 7:30 in the morning. Since they were the first items loaded into the truck, they were placed at the very front of the truck. Later, the truck was filled with automobile tires and batteries to be delivered to a gas station near Walker's store.

Harry spent all morning delivering the tires and batteries. He finished just before noon. Instead of driving over to Walker's store, Harry Verner decided to stop for lunch. It was very hot that day, so Harry parked the truck under a tree, hoping the shade would keep the truck cool. He finished lunch about one-thirty and drove straight over to Walker's Market.

When Mr. Walker came out of the store, he said it was too late to sell Halloween candy since trick or treating would start in just a few hours. Harry said that it wasn't his fault the candy came in late. After all, he'd just picked it up from the warehouse that morning.

Harry began unloading the sixteen cases of candy. He soon discovered that most of the boxes of candy were warm and that some of them were even dripping chocolate.

When Mr. Walker saw the mess, he refused to pay Harry the money he owed him for delivering the candy. He said he wasn't going to pay for late and damaged merchandise. Harry said that if Mr. Walker ordered the candy, then he had to pay for it. When Mr. Walker refused, Harry called the police. Now the case is in court.

Make a list of the arguments you might use to support Harry's position. Then make a list of the arguments that you would use to defend Mr. Walker. When you are finished, write a script that demonstrates what this case might sound like if it were before a judge.

May

June

Flags Aloft

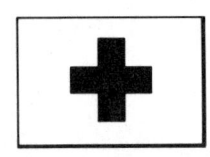

13 STAR 1777 FLAG   **15 STAR 1795 FLAG**   **TODAY'S 50 STAR FLAG**   **OLYMPIC FLAG**   **RED CROSS FLAG**

What do Betsy Ross, George Washington, and Francis Hopkinson have in common?

All three of these people at one time or another have been credited with designing the first American flag. Some people believe that Betsy Ross designed and sewed the first flag. According to an old family legend, Betsy Ross — a Philadelphia seamstress — was visited in 1775 by a secret committee. The committee (which supposedly included George Washington) asked Ross to create a flag for Washington's headquarters.

Some historians argue that it was Washington who designed the flag that first flew in front of his Massachusetts headquarters in the winter of 1776. These historians believe that not until several months later did Washington and Francis Hopkinson visit Mrs. Ross and ask her to copy Washington's design.

Francis Hopkinson, however, was heard to tell still another version of the story. Hopkinson was a New Jersey lawyer, painter, author, and musician. He was also one of the signers of the Declaration of Independence. He claimed to friends that he designed the flag. Regardless of who actually designed it, the first American flag did serve to guide the Revolutionary soldiers to victory and independence for the new country.

On June 14, 1777, Congress formally adopted a flag of thirteen alternating red and white stripes (representing the original thirteen states) with thirteen white stars on a blue background as the first official flag of the United States. Since the first design was adopted, the United States flag has been changed many times. Flag designs are changed with the changing face of a country. Think of a flag design that might represent your city as you become the director of Flags Aloft.

Flags Aloft

Name _____

Flags Aloft

A FEW FLAG FACTS: The colors, shape, and design of a flag all have some significance for the people of the country. Just as the stars on the U.S. flag represent the individual states, the eagle and cactus on the flag of Mexico represent the struggle for independence. State and city flags also use symbols, shape, and color to convey a message. You have been asked to design a flag to represent the city in which you live. Design the flag below, and then explain your design. Remember, everything placed on the flag must have some significance.

What colors did you use on the flag? _____

What shape is this flag? _____

What symbols, designs, or patterns did you include on the flag? _____
_____

Using these lines and other paper, write a description of your flag, including the reasons you had for designing it the way you did.

_____
_____
_____
_____
_____
_____
_____
_____

June

June

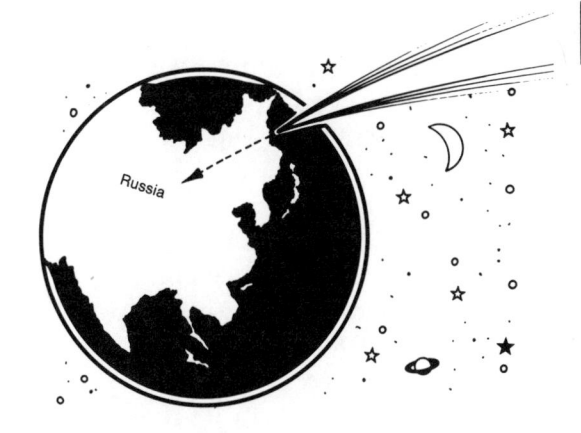

Flashdown!

Here is one of life's unsolved mysteries:

In June 1908, something large struck the earth with a terrific impact. Years later, scientists still do not have the explanation.

On the morning of the mysterious explosion, the Eskimos living at the Vanovera trading station in Siberia looked up to see a flaming mass streaking toward Earth. What appeared to be steam and particles of dust trailed behind the fireball for miles. When the fireball hit the Earth in the Tunguska River basin, the blast threw the Eskimos to the ground. Others, caught closer to the basin, reported being lifted several feet into the air on a blanket of blistering heat.

People living as far as 600 miles from the point of impact reported hearing a loud explosion followed by other strange sounds. Entire forests were suddenly destroyed. All of the fallen trees pointed away from the center of the blast as if they had been pushed rather than pulled from the ground. Scientists immediately began to collect as much evidence as they could, trying to find a logical explanation for what had happened.

When the Russian scientist E.L. Krilov and his assistants arrived to study the explosion, they were immediately faced with a mystery. Dozens of witnesses reported seeing an object streaking through the sky, and even more reported feeling the ground beneath them shake when the object crashed. But when Dr. Krilov examined the area, he could find no crater. There was no evidence that anything had actually landed on the Earth at all.

More than three-quarters of a century have passed since the Tunguska Fireball was spotted. But still no scientist has ever been able to solve the mystery of what happened in Siberia that June day. Perhaps you will have better luck explaining another of life's unsolved mysteries.

Flashdown!

Flashdown!

Name _____

DEDUCING DINOSAURS' DISAPPEARANCE: For almost 150,000,000 years, dinosaurs ruled the earth. They ranged in size from the relatively small Thecodant to the sixty-ton Supersaurus. But regardless of their size, they all disappeared more than sixty-three million years ago. Below you will read some information about what the Earth was like shortly before the dinosaurs' death. Using this information, along with some of the theories scientists have developed to explain the mysterious disappearance, come up with your own theory about what happened to the dinosaurs millions of years ago...

1. Sixty-three million years ago the climate on Earth was relatively warm.
2. There were forests, deserts, and deep woods. Plants grew even near the Arctic Circle at the top of the world.
3. Dinosaurs lived in many lands. Some of them were carnivores — meat-eating creatures that even ate fellow dinosaurs. Other dinosaurs were herbivores, depending on the lush plants for their daily food supply.
4. Most of the dinosaurs were land-dwelling creatures, although scientists have found skeletons of flying dinosaurs as well as dinosaurs that lived most of their lives in the deep ocean waters.

BUT THEN, OVER A PERIOD OF JUST A FEW MILLION YEARS, THE DINOSAURS DISAPPEARED.
1. Some scientists believe a giant meteor struck Earth, covering the entire planet with a heavy layer of dust that blocked out the sun. This sudden darkness caused all of the plant life to die, and the dinosaurs starved to death.
2. Others believe that some new disease spread over the globe killing nearly all of the prehistoric animals.

You are now the scientist researching the dinosaurs' plight. Use magazine articles, encyclopedias, and other resources in your library to learn what might have happened millions of years ago. When you finish your research, write a short explanation of what you think happened to the dinosaurs. This statement is called a "theory." After you've written your theory, summarize the reasons why you feel your theory may truly explain what happened to the dinosaurs.

YOUR THEORY _____

_____

_____

Use another sheet of paper to summarize all of the information you found which supports your theory. Be sure to list the title of each book, magazine, or filmstrip from which you took information.

June

June

A Summer Time Capsule

Why does a grandfather clock run more slowly on warm days?

SLOOOOOOWWW

Does this question sound like the beginning of a complicated riddle? Actually the answer is a simple scientific fact. Metals expand as they get warmer, and the metal pendulum of a grandfather clock is no exception. As the days grow warmer, the pendulum grows slightly larger, forcing it to move more slowly.

The slowing of a clock's movement is just one example of the many changes that take place as summer approaches. People talk about the days getting longer. There are still just twenty-four hours in each day, but a greater number of those hours are spent in daylight. The longest day of the year falls on either June 20 or 21. That date, known as the "summer solstice," also marks the first day of summer.

During the summer, most people change the way they spend their days. Almost everyone begins to spend more time living, playing, and working outside. Many cities offer recreational activities in parks. Beaches, swimming pools, and miniature golf courses reopen for the warm months. Families often schedule vacations during the summer.

Everyone looks forward to doing special things during the summer. Give some thought to your summer plans as you begin to write A Summer Time Capsule.

A Summer Time Capsule

Name _____

A Summer Time Capsule

CAPSULE COMMENTS: For centuries, people have buried things and thoughts about their past, their present, and their hopes for the future in time capsules. A capsule can be constructed of almost any material and can be stored in any convenient place. It is fun to list certain things you want to happen in the future, and then store the list away until that future time has come and gone. Using the time capsule guide below, list your summer plans, explaining where, when and why you want to do them. Then store the list in a safe place until next September. You'll probably be surprised at how much both you and your plans will have changed in just a few months.

TIME CAPSULE GUIDE

Today's Date _____

Date this time capsule is to be opened _____

My height today _____

My weight today _____

My best friend(s) today _____
_____

This summer's recreational plans (explain when, where, and why):
_____
_____
_____
_____

This summer's travel plans: _____
_____
_____
_____

This summer's hobby plans: _____
_____

Signature _____

June